Further Praise for Th

M000006961

"Steve Nobel's book takes you on a journey through the labyrinths of scarcity as they manifest in the world of work and money, and will bring you out into the light of possibility, grace and prosperity."
—Nick Williams, author of *The Work We Were Born To Do*, and founder of Heart at Work, London"

"I have never been interested in the subject of money, but very interested in my belief in the lack of it. Steve Nobel's book has enriched me into a better way of thinking. An informative and enjoyable journey through a well-written book."
—Becky Walsh Presenter of The Psychic Show on LBC 97.3 radio

"Steve Nobel has written an in-depth and fascinating account of how a person moves from the mundane and painful world of scarcity to the ABUNDANT world of inner and outer riches."
—Alberto Villoldo, author of *Shaman, Healer, Sage*

"Steve Nobel, in his unique masterful way, has weaved a magical carpet using the threads of spirituality, mythology, art, quantum mechanics, ecology, human behaviour and taken us on a journey from our deepest fears of lack to an enlightened understanding of ourselves and our relationship with abundance."
—Sangeeta Sah, M.D,

THE PROSPERITY GAME

The Wealthy Way of Heart, Mind and Spirit

Steve Nobel

FINDHORN Press

© Steve Nobel 2006

The right of Steve Nobel to be identified as the author of this work
has been asserted by him in accordance with the
Copyright, Designs and Patents Act 1998.

First published by Findhorn Press 2006

ISBN 10: 1-84409-080-9
ISBN 13: 978-1-84409-080-8

All rights reserved. The contents of this book may not be reproduced in any
form, except for short extracts for quotation or review, without the written
permission of the publisher.

British Library Cataloguing-in-Publication Data.
A catalogue record for this book is available from the British Library.

Edited by Kate Keogan
Cover design by Damian Keenan
Interior design by Pam Bochel
Printed and bound by WS Bookwell, Finland

1 2 3 4 5 6 7 8 9 10 11 12 13 12 11 10 09 08 07 06

Published by
Findhorn Press
305A The Park,
Findhorn, Forres
Scotland IV36 3TE

Tel 01309 690582
Fax 01309 690036
email: info@findhornpress.com
www.findhornpress.com

Contents

Introduction

Life is a game of amazing diversity. In this world we can experience fabulous wealth, terrible poverty, or something in between. In some parts of the world the game is played with tremendous struggle and hardship. In other places it is played with a lot of competing and striving. Both lead to great unhappiness.

Some people have few material assets yet manage to experience great joy. Others have accumulated considerable material wealth yet feel bored and unhappy. A glorious few manage to live both a happy and successful life. These are the ones playing the prosperity game. This book is about learning to play such a game.

Scarcity and prosperity are words which describe activities and attitudes: they are not physical things. They are not something which we can put onto a table and examine. They cannot be adjusted or fixed like machines. We are not handed a certain quota of either at birth. They denote internal attitudes which we hold (consciously or unconsciously) from moment to moment which lead to external activities and consequences. Scarcity and prosperity manifest through our attitudes, beliefs, habits, thoughts, and feelings, before they appear in the world. Scarcity and prosperity are self-perpetuating games that we choose to play.

Scarcity is a game that is played at many different levels, from the personal all the way up to the global. It is a game maintained by false promises, penalties and punishments as well as a lack of real and enduring values. Scarcity gives importance to fleeting, fashionable things and even to deadly things. It gives hardly any to important things or things which are truly enjoyable and sustainable.

This book's contention is that every problem in the world has at its core some issue of scarcity. We can experience a scarcity of money, opportunity, time, caring, freedom, happiness, peace or purpose. Scarcity creates a scary world. Scarcity seeks to solve the problems it creates through striving and playing harder and faster. This strategy leads us ever more deeply into scarcity. In this book we will explore scarcity and how it plays out through money, work and the world in which we live.

Prosperity is a whole different game, with a whole different mindset. Prosperity is a conversation, a way of thinking and feeling, a deep connection with life. Here are a few pointers to get you going:

1. Prosperity is a game that can be played by anyone. To begin, all you need is the willingness to participate. Any book, course or teacher will only be of use to the degree in which you actively participate with the material offered. Your involvement is the real magic that creates the transformation.

2. The more you are able to lighten up and play the more fun you will have and the better your results will be. A game is not meant to be played too seriously. Scarcity has been played far too seriously across the planet for too long.

3. This game is a mirror. What you see on the outside is a clue to the game you are playing on the inside. The reflection in the mirror changes when you change on the inside. When you transform scarcity in yourself you will literally see, hear and touch a different world.

4. You have been conditioned to play this game from the outside in. Scarcity conditioning needs to be reversed so that you start to play from the inside out. When you awaken to prosperity consciousness you will naturally feel richer on the inside and also, in time, on the outside.

5. As you play with the possibilities of prosperity you cannot help but touch others around you. Your prosperity play will assist and inspire others. As you play to assist others to be more prosperous you cannot avoid being rewarded yourself.

6. This game will take you on a journey that will engage your latent conscious and unconscious resources. Inner and outer resources will spontaneously become available as you engage in this play. You will awaken to your spiritual resources and create a relationship with the Higher Intelligence within the game.

7. Playing the game will help you heal the age-old split between spirit and matter. You play to experience both material and spiritual richness. In this game, inner and outer riches are not mutually exclusive. There is no end to the possibilities you can create and experience in this game.

Do you want to come and play?
Hope so!

Love and blessings,
Steve Nobel

Part One

Scarcity = The Way of

Lack and Misery

Chapter 1

Scarcity = Money-Centred Living

The greed for fruit misses the flower.

RABINDRANATH TAGORE

Many years ago there lived a king named Midas who was very, very rich; it was said that he had more gold than any other king in the world. The king grew so fond of his gold that he eventually loved it better than anything else in the entire world. His one great wish was for more and more gold and one day, while he was in his gold room counting his money, a beautiful fairy boy stood before him. The boy's face shone with a wonderful light, and in his hand he carried a strange-looking wand.

'Midas, you are the richest man in the world,' said the young fairy. 'There is no king who has as much gold as you.'

'That may be,' said the king. 'As you see, I have this room full of gold, but I should like much more.'

'Are you sure?' asked the fairy.

'I am very sure,' answered the king.

'If I should grant you one wish,' said the fairy, 'would you ask for more gold?'

'If I could have but one wish,' said the king, 'I would ask that everything I touch should turn to gold.'

'Your wish shall be granted,' said the fairy. 'At sunrise tomorrow your slightest touch will turn everything into gold. But I warn you that your gift will not make you happy.'

'I will take the risk,' said the king.

Principle One   *Scarcity-thinking says that money buys confidence, freedom, happiness and self-worth. It says that the point of life is to accumulate, consume, strive and spend.*

Scarcity = A False Premise

In the capitalist world there is the general assumption that if we produce more and more services and products then we will all automatically become collectively happier. This rather simple model for happiness has meant that money has become the measure of all things important to us. Our very existence is thus ascertained in terms of the amount of euros, dollars, sterling or yen we possess. It is from such an idea that scarcity is born.

We all live in a world of scarcity. We might not be able to see or touch it but scarcity touches us everyday. Scarcity moves through the global money markets, it is seated at corporate board meetings and is debated by governments. It moves through family systems and shows up in conflict. It stares out at us through the stories and imagery of glossy magazines and it is reported daily in the newspapers. Scarcity affects both rich and poor alike. It snakes through the underbelly of our cities and through the underclass in the streets. Children are born into it and adults struggle endlessly with it. Scarcity is intangible and deadly.

Scarcity is like the story of the computer hologram in The Matrix. It is an invisible world that surrounds us but which we do not realize is there. We have to be told about it to experience it for ourselves. Only then can we unplug from it. Scarcity is the feeling that there is something wrong with the world. It is an invisible prison forged within the mind. Being in this prison means that we can never really be who we are and live to our full capability. Once we really understand that we are being held in a prison of scarcity, everything changes. Nothing can remain the same anymore. Our modern world has so much to offer; it is easy to disbelieve that scarcity is a part of modern living. Yet nothing that the modern world has to offer can free us from scarcity. Every glittering product or amazing service has the potential to take us deeper into the prison of scarcity. Scarcity is a state of mind that colours and influences all of our outer experiences. In the state of scarcity, no amount of money, houses, holidays or sexual encounters will give a sense of deep fulfilment or lasting happiness. Each purchase or experience gives but a temporary release from its grip. Most of us have become so deeply infused with scarcity consciousness that we are blind to it.

Scarcity is a voracious and all-pervading feeling of lack. It comes from the belief that there is not enough in the world – not enough money, love, happiness… the list is endless. Scarcity has many ways of touching us but perhaps its most profound method is through the ways in which we think and feel about, and relate to, money.

Scarcity is a lack of not only money but of every resource imaginable. It is a strangulation of living where the importance of hope and possibility diminish in favour of security and money. The word 'economics' is derived from the Ancient Greek word meaning 'home', and the home is where we create and nurture life. Scarcity is not much concerned with the home for it is a death grip – a world of hungry ghosts, starving children and criminal greed. Scarcity finds solace in every couple who argue over money and every workplace that has a 'nose to the grindstone' mentality. Scarcity is found between a rock and a hard place; it is a place of great emptiness, although not in the Zen sense. This kind of emptiness is the feeling of never being fulfilled, satisfied or complete. Scarcity is like a bath with the plug always out; no matter how much water is poured in, the bath can never be full. The water just runs away.

In the scarcity mindset, money is linked to issues of survival. When this is so, considerable emotion becomes attached to it. Our attitude of scarcity keeps us worrying about our bills or diminishing savings. It takes our mind away from what we want to do with our lives or for others and reduces our life to a bank statement. When we have money, we can breathe easy, we have kept the creditors from the door. When we have little money, it is as though the very air that we breathe is in short supply. We start to breathe shallowly and focus on all manner of nightmarish scenarios. We need money in order to live, but linking money to survival like this keeps us playing very small in life and locked in a prison of our own making.

In the scarcity mindset, money equals power: the power of greater personal choice and opportunity. Money as power can also translate into having more power to control and manipulate others. Parents can manipulate their children and bosses can manipulate their workers through the promise of more money or the threat of its withdrawal.

The scarcity mentality gives money the power to build or destroy friendships, to enhance or crumble self-esteem. It determines how a relationship begins, continues and ends. Money can sustain or topple nations.

In this scarcity mindset, money equals love. Parents give money to their children as a substitute for love. In some relationships, the amount of money lavished on a partner is an indicator of the amount of love felt for that person. It is a strange thing that money can't buy us love but a diamond is somehow still a girl's best friend. Money can't buy us love but it can help us get a higher degree of sexual attention!

In the scarcity mindset, money equals self-worth: the more money we have, the more worthy we are. The problem is that when we spend or lose money, we are spending or losing our self-worth. Our monthly salary then determines how worthy we feel. In the scarcity mindset, money is an indicator of success. The more successful (so the thinking goes), the bigger the house, the grander the office, the more stylish the mobile phone and the more expensive the clothes. Success in the scarcity mindset is thus measured solely by material things.

Scarcity is a game that we play in which our lives are speeding up. We need to work ever harder and more quickly for our money. Money has become a central issue in many people's lives: how to get enough of it and how to keep hold of more of it. Other meaningful things, such as family, friendships and life purpose get shoved to one side.

When money becomes the centre of our lives, we become money addicts. Money addicts are always on the lookout for the next money fix. There is no peace of mind for the money addict: there are only moments of distraction, fantasy and anxiety about having enough. The money addict is locked into a cycle of craving ever more. This craving can never be satisfied. Living in a world of money addiction means living in a world of never having enough and of craving what we do not have. Thus, scarcity makes the accumulation and spending of money the core purpose of life.

Some people have far too little desire for money. They decide that money is not important and relegate it to the edges of their lives. This is just as problematic as putting it in the centre. The denial of money is the flip side of money addiction. Some people hate money and project all of their problems on to it. Some people hate money because they think that it is evil, dirty and a corrupting force. Some people with strong spiritual values believe that it is not possible to be spiritually and materially successful and thus keep money at a great distance. All of these attitudes keep us playing the scarcity game.

Scarcity keeps us playing small and holds us in the place of defending our small gains. Scarcity is a form of harsh accountancy where we keep profit and loss sheets on every activity in life. The scarcity mindset believes that such things as appreciation, creativity, community, generosity and kindness do not always readily convert into hard cash and so may be dismissed as a foolish waste of time.

King Midas was a wealthy man who foolishly craved more wealth. After his wish was granted, everything he touched turned to gold. All the food and drink he tried to consume turned to gold so that he grew pale and thin. All the flowers in his garden turned to gold when he brushed against them. Soon, his whole palace and estates were transformed into gold. People learnt to avoid him for fear of being turned into gold. When he accidentally turned his beloved daughter to gold, he started to pray fervently for deliverance. History has many such 'Midas' stories. In 1774, the Austrian princess Marie Antoinette married the Dauphin, who in time became King Louis XVI of France. She was beautiful, vivacious and strong-minded. She supported her husband's alliance with the American Colonials in their fight for independence from Britain. This almost bankrupted France. She persuaded her husband to raise taxes to pay for her expensive lifestyle and to renovate her luxurious Palace at Versailles. At a time when most of the population was out of work and queuing in bread-lines, she was daubed 'Madame Deficit' by the common people. In 1793, Marie Antoinette met her end at the guillotine in Paris.

Scarcity is like that. It promises much but is really leading us to an unhappy ending. Scarcity creates vampire-like individuals and corporations which suck the life force out of anyone foolish enough to get too close. When a business operates from a scarcity mentality, it will foolishly and irresponsibly run up debts and eventually go out of business. A government with a scarcity mindset will behave covertly, corruptly and even criminally. At a global level, scarcity is truly frightening; it will create extreme wealth for a few and great misery for many.

Scarcity = A Money-Mad World

A woman was told that she had only six months to live.

She asked her doctor, 'What shall I do?'

'Marry an accountant,' was the doctor's advice.

'Will that make me live longer?' asked the woman.

'No, but it will seem longer!'

The trouble with money is not really a question of how much or how little there is of it in the world but of how well or poorly it is created, distributed, and put to use. We may feel that we must lie, cheat and steal for it, feel ashamed or guilty about it, or sell our soul to have more of it. We may hate or love money, and blame it for our past and present circumstances.

Yet we live in a world where there is no shortage of money. Billions of dollars are held in and flow through offshore tax havens. Billions of dollars worth of assets are owned by the top corporations across the world. Every day, billions of dollars are moved around the world through the world money markets. There is no shortage of money in the world but this has not decreased the number of problems that we collectively face in the world.

Have you ever had the thought that, if you had an unlimited supply of money, all your problems would be over? Many people have won a lot of money and found that, far from solving their problems, it created a lot more. Evelyn Adams won the New Jersey lottery not just once but twice to the tune of several millions. Today, the money is all gone and Adams lives in a trailer. Janite Lee won millions and was very generous to a variety of causes, particularly politics, education and the community. But, within a few years of her win, she had filed for bankruptcy.

It is strange but true that around £15 billion sits in unclaimed accounts in the U.K. It is mainly attributed to people dying and the money being forgotten about or, even more strangely, when money is deposited and then forgotten while the owner is still alive. In the U.S. around $9billion in savings bonds remains unclaimed.

Scarcity = A World of Debt

Scarcity creates a world of debt. Debt is the price we pay for living in a consumerist society that is founded on borrowing. Debt keeps people slaving in order to maintain their debts and overdrafts. Debt is a black hole into which many people fall and it arises in many ways – unemployment, bad luck speculating, a failed business, negative equity in the housing market, living beyond our means and so on. Debt affects old and young. Some people cannot face debt and tragically decide instead to end their lives.

Debt is crippling many developing nations even though many have already paid back their original debts many times over. Crisis sets in when interest rates skyrocket and compound interest makes repayment practically impossible. Debt repayments are keeping many developing nations from providing their citizens with access to clean water, adequate housing or basic health care.

It is not just poor nations that are in debt. In the UK in 2004, our collective personal debt broke through the £1 trillion barrier.[1]

Scarcity = A World of Injustice

Today, the mega-rich have been accumulating fortunes on a scale and at a pace not seen for close to a century. This trend is not so much the result of successful business creation as of increased levels of personal enrichment from speculation and corporate wheeling and dealing. Twenty years ago, the average chief executive of a FTSE 100 company earned around 25 times that of an average worker: today, it is closer to 120 times.[2]

It is a strange sign of the times that rewards for failure have become quite commonplace in the corporate world. In the UK, agreements which guarantee large payouts to out-going company executives are known as 'golden parachutes'. In the U.S., they are called 'golden condoms' because they protect the shareholder and screw the company.

Money has somehow crept into the very heart of how people live their lives. Money can be a cruel dictator. What was once an excellent servant has become a poor master.

Scarcity generates corruption, injustice and financial waste. There are a number of dictators around the world who have stolen billions from their countries. For instance, it is estimated that President Suharto of Indonesia stole as much as $35 billion from Indonesia during his three decades in power. President Marcos of the Philippines is estimated to have stolen around $10 billion of the $26 billion of foreign aid given to his country during his presidency. It is thought that President Mobutu Seko of Zaire – now the Democratic Republic of Congo – stole almost half of the $12 billion in aid money that his country received from the IMF during his 32-year reign. It is estimated that Slobodan Milosevic siphoned away $1 billion from Serbia between 1972 and 1986.[3]

Corruption is not just the privilege of presidents: sometimes whole countries get in on the act. In 1988, Russia was granted a $4.8 billion loan by the International Monetary Fund; most of it mysteriously disappeared almost as soon as it arrived, via a series of anonymous offshore finance channels.[4] These moneys were placed in foreign banks and then used to loan back to the developing countries.

According to a report by the African Union, corruption costs Africa nearly $150 billion per year.[5] From the bribe of a bottle of whisky slipped under the counter to speed up a traveller's passage through customs, to the president living way beyond his declared means, corruption increases the cost of goods by as much as 20%, as well as deterring investment and holding back development. Most of the cost, the report says, falls on the poor.

Changing Your Money Game

The outer scarcity game is played within each one of us. This may seem hard to believe at first yet scarcity did not arise by itself, it was birthed from somewhere and that somewhere was us and continues to be us. Scarcity is a mistake that has arisen in our response to life. It rages daily in our own thoughts and feelings and physical responses. Understanding the outer game is useful because it gives us clues to our inner game.

We have internalized the scarcity game, whether we like it or not, and we must undo it from the inside out. Until we address our inner game, nothing much will change in the external world. The rules of the inner scarcity game are determined by what we believe is possible or desirable regarding money. To change our relationship with money, we need to begin by getting honest. Honesty combined with compassion is a good formula for changing our game.

Keeping a Prosperity Journal

To work with the exercises in this book you will need a prosperity journal – an A4 (US Letter) or A5 blank notebook in which to record your journey and note the exercises. Your first task is to go out and buy one.

This is important to track your progress through the book. Please date your entries so that you can note your challenges and insights in relation to a time scale.

Start in your journal by noting your thoughts and feelings about the nature of scarcity. How does all that you have read about scarcity in the world touch you? How does it reflect your own issues of scarcity? How do you keep playing the scarcity game?

Please do not censor any thought or feeling. Allow your feelings to inform your writing.

Journal Work ~ Scarcity and Money

What messages did you receive about money from your parents?

What messages about money did you receive from your peers, bosses, teachers?

What do you like and dislike about money?

To what degree do you believe that money can solve all of your problems?

What do you make money mean? Is it confidence, happiness, success?

What do you think about rich people?

What do you think about poor people?

If you have debts, how do you feel about them?

How does money stop you from doing what you want to do?

Note all your responses in your journal.

Please do not censor any thought or feeling.
Allow your feelings to move your writing.
Please keep your journal private.

References

1. http://news.bbc.co.uk/1/hi/business/3935671.stm
2. http://www.taxjustice.net/cms/front_content.php?idcat=29
3. http://www.guardian.co.uk/international/story/0,3604,1178342,00.html
4. http://www.mega.nu/ampp/communism1.html
5. http://news.bbc.co.uk/1/hi/world/africa/2265387.stm

Chapter 2

Scarcity = Lack at Work

Old Mother Hubbard
Went to the cupboard
To get her poor doggie a bone,
When she got there
The cupboard was bare
So the poor little doggie had none.

BRITISH NURSERY RHYME

In Ancient Greek mythology there is the story of a timber merchant called Erisychthon who thought only of his personal profit. He cut down every tree he could find for money; no tree was safe from his axe. Then he came across a grove that was sacred to the Gods, and in the grove was a sacred oak whose boughs were bedecked with wreaths, each containing many prayers. Everyone held this tree to be holy yet none of this mattered to Erisychthon. As he lifted his axe to cut down the tree, the spirit of the sacred tree spoke out in loud protest. Yet this did not stop him from cutting her down. News of this sacrilege reached the ears of Ceres, goddess of abundance and fertility. She put a curse on Erisychthon for his greed and contempt. He was cursed with a 'hurricane of starvation' and from that day on he was gripped with an insatiable hunger that held him in a frenzy. He began to eat everything he could find, and when he had eaten everything he could get his hands on he converted all of his wealth into food. When he had eaten everything his wealth could buy he ate his wife and children. Finally, when there was nothing left, he ate himself.

Principle Two   *The scarcity mindset is present in the ways in*
which we earn money. Work that is boring,
meaningless or stressful is the work of scarcity.

Scarcity = A Dog-Eat-Dog World

The first series of the BBC comedy *The Office* was first shown in 2001. It was a resounding success. The second series was viewed by around 5 million people in the UK and went on to be a cult success on BBC America. *The Office* was a painfully humourous portrayal of some of the antics, misery and boredom of office life. It shows how scarcity has long been rife in the world of work. Scarcity creates a dog-eat-dog world where nation, company, and individual find themselves fighting in a fiercely competitive marketplace. The fight here is for capturing trade and securing profit; it is little wonder that the world of work sometimes resembles a military zone. At work many people find that they must work increasingly hard and more quickly. At the same time, many complain of losing a sense of meaning and purpose for what they are doing. Work becomes a vehicle for scarcity when it becomes a series of tasks performed purely and simply for financial reward. Scarcity at work leads to our being on the hamster wheel of boredom, busyness, hard work and stress. Wherever work is a daily slog, rather than a daily joy, the scarcity game is in operation. Scarcity at work results in an empty, grey, monotonous landscape where we have lost touch with the parts of ourselves that are naturally creative, hopeful, funny, focused, sensitive, resourceful, powerful, and optimistic. This kind of work is anti-living.

Although there are jobs which require little initiative, thinking, innovation or creativity, if they take place in an atmosphere that is friendly and inviting they can feel delightful. On the other hand, some highly-skilled jobs take place in very dull and stupefying workplaces. Prosperity at work is ideally concerned with doing activities we love in an environment which feels joyful, friendly, stimulating and supportive.

Scarcity at work is about survival. Although work offers the potential for so much more than mere survival, the scarcity mindset finds this hard to appreciate. Scarcity at work keeps countless numbers of people locked into jobs that generate little interest or enthusiasm. Such jobs are damaging to their physical, emotional and mental health.

Scarcity = Busyness at Work

Scarcity is about busyness. During the 1960s there was the idea that, as we approached the 21st century, people would be enjoying more leisure time because improvements in technology would made work easier and shorter. The idea was that all the dull and mundane aspects of work would be eventually replaced by machines, and people would be freer to get on with the more important and meaningful things in life. Now that we are in the 21st century, this has clearly not happened. Victorian economists worked out that in 1495 a peasant had to work for 15 weeks of the year to earn the money needed to survive.[1] By 1564 it was 40 weeks. Now it is almost impossible in the UK for a family with children to survive on the wage of one parent working fulltime. We live in an overwork culture where many are literally working themselves to death. Here, time is money and all hours, minutes and seconds in the day can be bought and sold. We no longer pass the time: we spend it. Not only is our time spent at work but we spend time commuting. Once at work, many endure long working hours.

There is a thin line between being busy and being a workaholic. Workaholics do not work to live, they live to work. Workaholics make work their number one priority and can devote as much as 16 hours a day working furiously, making money, and striving towards their goals. A workaholic will gradually forget the reason why they are working so hard. They will skip meals in order to get things done; they will cut down on the time they spend resting or sleeping and they will blur all distinctions between work and home life. It is a sad fact that work intrudes into around a million bedrooms in the UK via pagers, bleepers and mobile phones 24/7.

Scarcity = Boredom and Stress

A man was given the job of painting white lines down the middle of the road. On his first day he painted six miles; on his second day, three miles; and on his third day, one mile.

The foreman was not pleased. He asked the worker, 'How come you're doing less each day?'

'Because each day I get further away from the paint can,' came the reply.

Scarcity creates boring work. One survey found that 1 in 3 people had taken drugs such as ecstasy, cocaine and cannabis whilst at work.[2] In another , one in four admitted to falling asleep in the workplace.[3] People who are enthused by their work do not take drugs or fall asleep whilst doing it!

Boring work is an endemic problem. Some people do not believe that they are capable or worthy of juicy work and so settle for less. Some people do believe that they are capable and worthy and go for their career goals. After achieving these goals, they sometimes reach a plateau where money might be flowing in but there is a lack of new dreams and goals to stretch for. Such people have a low boredom threshold. They need ongoing challenge, learning and development in their chosen field, otherwise they are just plain unhappy. One high flying executive felt that he had reached the pinnacle of success. But when a colleague asked him how he was doing he turned to say, 'Fine,' and instead collapsed on the floor, sobbing. In that moment he realized that he was not happy doing what he was doing. This story is not unfamiliar amongst high flyers, intelligent and highly skilled people. Some people in other jobs just reach a point where they feel bored, unmotivated and unproductive. Boredom is as much a trap as overwork. Most companies with a scarcity mindset seek to employ people in a job for which they already have a proven track record. This is a recipe for general boredom and unhappiness. It does not offer any possibility for a development of untapped potential. Where work does not help us to become more of who we are, where it does not teach us new things about ourselves and life, where it is done for just the money, then it will be probably bore us to death.

Scarcity is about stress and overwork. When we are overly busy at work, our leisure time is merely spent in resting and recovering from overwork. According to research conducted by the Health and Safety Executive, about half a million people in the UK experience work-related stress at a level which they believe is making them ill. Up to 5 million people in the UK feel 'very' or 'extremely' stressed by their work. The result is that around 13.4 million working days each year are lost due to stress, costing the UK over £3.7 billion annually.[4]

Stress can be caused by: excessive workloads; infrequent rest breaks; long working hours; hectic and routine tasks that have little inherent meaning; a lack of participation by workers in decision-making; poor communication within an organization; lack of support; a poor social environment; conflicting or uncertain job expectations; too many 'hats to wear'; job insecurity; lack of opportunity for growth or advancement; change for which workers are unprepared; unpleasant or dangerous physical conditions such as crowding, noise pollution, or ergonomic problems. Stress has also been implicated in a wide range of medical conditions such as depression, irritable bowel disease, back problems, headaches, high blood pressure, nervous problems, and ulcers. Stress mobilizes the body's fight or flight response; the heart rate increases, blood flow changes and sweat increases. When we feel unable to respond by running or fighting, this hyperactivity in the body on a continual basis generally leads to illness. Stress not only affects physical health; it can feel like a series of body blows to a person's dignity, self-esteem and mental and emotional ability to cope in the world.

Scarcity = Bullying

In 1994, a survey indicated that half of all employees have been bullied at work during their working life.[5] Another survey found that 1 in 8 (around 3 million) UK employees had been bullied in the workplace in the previous five years.[6] Bullying happens in extremely competitive environments, or where there is a fear of redundancy or a fear for one's position. It happens in the context of authoritarian styles of management, excessive organizational change or excessive workloads. Bullying can take the form of verbal abuse, public humiliation, excessively tight supervision, persistent and undue criticism, undermining of responsibility, being excluded from social gatherings, malicious gossiping, or even physical and sexual intimidation. Bullying flourishes when people feel that they would rather put up with abusive behaviour from bosses and colleagues than confront the issue or leave the job.

The cycle of stress – chasing money to ease the stress of having to earn money to ease the stress – is like a cat chasing its own tail. This can also have an impact within the family. The parent that comes home from a hard day's work may have little energy to give to their family. The stressed worker may not be able to express their anger and frustration at work and so vent it within the home.

Changing Your Game at Work

In his *Inferno*, Dante speaks of being lost in a dark wood. He is unsure how he got there (and thinks he must have fallen asleep) but the experience is terrifying. He could so easily have been describing the world of scarcity at work. When scarcity is at play within the workplace, work will feel meaningless. It will feel boring, depressing or frantic, rather than exhilarating and fulfilling.

Scarcity says a job is about making money. Scarcity is not interested in things like growth or passion. Scarcity is not really interested in living an abundant life. Scarcity thinks about the next high, the next exciting purchase or holiday. Scarcity is not interested in our long term happiness or well-being, it is interested in short term gain. Scarcity thinking keeps people locked in jobs they have little affinity with.

Scarcity reduces work solely to making money. Work is meant to be so much more than this. Work can help us to find a sense of belonging, meaning and purpose in the world. It can help us to feel embedded in a meaningful community. Work can become part of the greater picture of a compelling and enjoyable life.

Boring, frantic or meaningless work demands a repression of who we truly are and keeps us from finding our highest destiny. This kind of work does not allow for any real creativity and does not allow us to explore our hidden, untapped potential. It may seem more comfortable to keep on doing a job that is safe yet boring or stressful but, in the long run, this kind of work erodes our natural zest and can be debilitating.

It is hard to know just how many people feel unhappy or uninterested in the jobs they do. This is perhaps one of the greatest tragedies of modern day living. Work does not have to be meaningless – it can be meaningful. Work need not feel boring, depressing or frantic. Work can generate incredible possibilities and feel exhilarating and fulfilling.

Engaging in the world of work is different from having a job. A job is often mundane, mechanical, political, joyless and hard. It can feel like a personal sacrifice or a selling of the soul for money. A job is usually done without much thinking or skill. Work on the other hand is something that engages our unique abilities and passions. Work is about creativity and it is usually a joy to do.

Why do you do the work you do? Do you have a natural passion and affinity for it? Or is it something that you do just for the money? Do you believe that you have to keep doing work that you feel little pleasure in doing? Do you feel that it is possible to raise your game and do something different?

Work is perhaps the greatest affirmation we give ourselves on a daily basis. Work demands the involvement of our physical, emotional and mental energies. Work can be a conduit for our spiritual energies. Work can draw us in the direction of new horizons or keep us paddling in the same shallow pool.

If your work is challenging, enjoyable and rewarding, it is an affirmation that is leading you more deeply into the prosperity game. If not, it is either holding you in a neutral place or leading you in the opposite direction, further into scarcity.

Work can become a source of pride when it is a means of positively touching and influencing the lives of others. It becomes a vehicle of incredible proportions if we make it a means of making a real and lasting difference to the planet. Can you imagine how it would feel if the work you did positively influenced the lives of hundreds or thousands of other people across the planet?

We live in a changing world, where there is no longer such a thing as a job for life. Prosperity at work is as much about growth, change and expanding into new ways of being as it is about earning money. Each one of us has a unique calling to do a certain kind of work. Scarcity thinking says that this is nonsense. Prosperity says that it is crucial to our ongoing growth and happiness.

Journal Work ~ Your Game at Work

Write briefly about the work that you do.

What do you most like about it?

What do you most dislike about it?

Does your work give you a sense of craftsmanship, satisfaction, direction and feeling of passion?

Does your work give you a sense of identity, belonging, knowing and purpose?

Do you feel radically alive in the work which you do?

Do you choose to continue doing this work?

If you had an unlimited amount of money, would you still be doing your current job?

If not, what kind of work would you choose to do instead?

What talents or skills would you like to liberate in your chosen work?

Do not censor any thoughts or emotions.

References

1. Boyle, David. *The Little Money Book*. Alistair Sawday Publishing, 2003
2. Time Out magazine, 2000
3. Reuters, 2004
4. http://www.management-issues.com/display_page.asp?section=research &id=624
5. Staffordshire University Business School, 1994
6. Institute of Personnel and Development, 1994

Chapter 3

Scarcity = Mass Insanity

There was a crooked man and he walked a crooked mile,
He found a crooked sixpence upon a crooked style.
He bought a crooked cat, which caught a crooked mouse,
And they all lived together in a little crooked house.

BRITISH NURSERY RHYME

Many years ago there lived an emperor who enjoyed fine clothes. One day two tailors presented themselves at the palace saying that they could create the finest suit of clothes for the emperor. They said that the cloth they used was of such wonderful quality that it could not be seen by anyone who was unpardonably stupid. The emperor was intrigued and delighted, and gave them a large sum of money to begin work. Time passed and the emperor grew increasingly impatient to see his new outfit of clothes. He decided to send a trusted minister to check on the progress of the tailors. The minister was invited into the room where the tailors cut and sewed the invisible cloth. No matter how hard the minister looked, he could not see the cloth. Not wishing to appear unpardonably stupid, he told them that he liked the pattern and colours of the cloth very much and he would tell the emperor that things were proceeding well. The tailors watched as the minister left and continued for a short while with their pretence of working with the invisible cloth.

Principle Three   *The scarcity mindset is a deadly and insane way of living that creates a world of lack, injustice and limitation.*

Scarcity = A World of Lack

The Hopi people of North America have the word *koyaanisquatsi* to describe our modern world. The word roughly translates as 'a world out of balance'. In a world of *koyaanisquatsi* we have war because of an over-abundance of fear and greed due to a lack of compassion and cooperation between nations. We have global pollution because of an over-abundance of get-rich-quick schemes, corporate greed and a scarcity of consideration and wisdom. We have family squabbles because of an over-abundance of anger and judgement and through a scarcity of love and real empathic communication.

Scarcity is at the core of everything that is wrong with the world in which we live. It is a virus that has infected the globe and we have all been infected by its touch. This is no-one's fault: it is just the way it is at the moment. Scarcity is ingrained in our emotional responses and in the way we think and behave. Scarcity is rampant across the planet and has infected our sophisticated global economies and scientific thinking, and is very present in the cut and thrust world of politics. Scarcity is a false idea, and the attempt to build prosperity on top of scarcity is to try and build a house on sand. Scarcity is the world we see through the distorted vision of the media – the world of bloodshed, conflict, corruption, disasters, greed, plague, starvation, and warfare. This world really does exist for many and is the consequence of living the lie of scarcity.

Scarcity motivates people out of self-interest and greed. Scarcity raises self-interest above our natural instinct to support and cooperate with each other. This guarantees that people will continue to feel an increasing sense of alienation, frustration and unhappiness. Self-interest alone is not the way to build a prosperous life. E. F. Schumacher, author of *Small is Beautiful* (Vintage, 1993) says that when societies are rife with these attitudes, they will fail to solve the most basic problems of daily life, in spite of their extraordinary achievements. Modern economics is based on the idea that there is not enough to go around. In the marketplace of supply and demand, scarce resources fetch a high price; according to modern economic theory, scarcity is a good thing. Hyping the demand for scarce resources is also seen as good in the eyes of many. Modern day marketing professionals are quite expert in getting people to buy things they have no real need or desire for.

Scarcity has made a god out of competition. Although competition can be a great thing if it motivates people to achieve, in the wrong spirit it is deadly. There is quite a difference between a friendly game of football where the aim is to play, win and have fun and a very serious game where the aim is to win at all costs even if that means physical injury to the opposing team. Here, competition becomes a fight – often with very unhappy consequences.

The scarcity mindset operates from the baseline assumption that happiness comes from having and misery comes from not having. It is with this in mind that the media bombard us with stories of the lives of the rich and famous. There is always someone giving advice on how to get more of what we want, and how to improve what we already have: our house, our finances or our love life. The restless search for more and the avoidance of less drives the world of scarcity.

Scarcity can adopt almost any system of thinking or theory to support its aims. For instance, Darwin's theory of evolution was a great breakthrough for its time; it provided an alternative to the Bible's view of creation. At the same time, industrial capitalism was growing, and some were looking for an ideology with which to justify its exploitation of the poor. Darwin's theory of natural selection was the answer; the idea of 'the survival of the fittest' became part of the rationale behind cut-throat capitalism.

Scarcity is the world of taking on a grand scale – both from the planet and from each other. Every day thousands of children starve from not having enough to eat while thousands of others become ill from eating too much of the wrong things. It is estimated that if everyone on the planet adopted a Western lifestyle, we would need five planets to support us. Around 20% of people living in the wealthy Western world consume 86% of the world's resources. The world's wealthiest 225 people have combined assets roughly equal to the annual income of the poorest 2.5 billion people.

Scarcity is a deadly game; it is the root cause of war. Most wars in history have been fought in order to obtain more resources or access to greater trade. War has always been a costly affair in terms of the destruction of property, land and human life. During the Great War of 1914-1918, not only were millions killed (Britain lost one million, France 1.7 million and Germany 2 million) but the total financial cost of the war for all sides amounted to over $126 billion.[1] After the war, the British Empire was on the verge of financial ruin because she had been forced to borrow large sums of money from America to continue the war effort. Financial hardships fuelled by the war were also a major factor in the Russian revolution of 1917. The heavy reparations imposed on defeated Germany (132 billion gold German marks) were a major factor in the economic collapse in Germany by 1922. Hyperinflation became so bad that people were forced to take wheelbarrows packed with money just to buy basic commodities. Economic problems were also among the fundamental causes that propelled Germany, Italy, and Japan into the Second World War. This war killed more people, cost more money, damaged more property, and affected more people in more countries than any other war in history.

Nowadays, war is an even more deadly and costly affair. To date, the U.S. has spent more than $5.5 trillion in developing its nuclear arsenal. Maintaining the current US nuclear arsenal of more than 10,000 warheads costs the U.S. taxpayer around $6.5 billion annually.[2] The cost of replacing the UK's four submarines armed with Trident missiles could reach £20 billion.[3] Today (2006), it is estimated that, globally, we spend almost $1,000 billion annually on military budgets.

Although we feel that we live in a 'civilized' world, beneath the surface of many peaceful activities a war is being waged in the name of scarcity. For instance, corporate globalization is sacrificing agricultural, cultural and economic diversity that has been around for thousands of years in return for high, short term financial gains. This is the scarcity game at its worst, seeking to override the intrinsic worth of plant and animal species, people and cultures in favour of get-rich-quick schemes. A free market economy sounds a wonderful thing but within the scarcity mindset it enables some nations to exploit trade rules at the expense of other nations. Scarcity seeks to profit through controlling markets. For instance, thirty companies now control a third of the world's processed food; five companies control 75% of the international grain trade; six companies manage 75% of the global pesticide market; two companies dominate sales of half the world's bananas; three companies trade 85% of the world's tea, and another controls 91% of the global GM seed market.[4] Now corporations have the power to set prices and influence international and domestic trade rules to suit themselves. This has not produced a world of plenty: quite the opposite. Here, owning means winning, whether these are tangible things like land and property or intangible things like 'intellectual rights' over ideas, information and music.

Scarcity is not only criminal, it is big business. Crime costs the world, not only through the resources it takes from the market but also in terms of the resources needed to police the world. Today, money laundering is measured in trillions rather than billions of dollars a year; the annual profits from drug trafficking is estimated to be as high as $500 billion a year. In the UK, the illegal drugs trade accounts for about £8.5 billion a year. Apart from oil and arms, the biggest world industries are now drugs, sex and illegal immigration. The annual revenue of the global prostitution business alone is worth around $52 billion. Organized crime has embraced globalization every bit as enthusiastically as have the heads of multi-national corporations. It is a disturbing fact that the total Gross Criminal Product is currently about 20% of total world trade.[5]

Scarcity = An Insane Game

In the world around us, people experience all kinds of lack: enough money, affordable housing; good medical care; time; energy; fun; laughter; love; joy or freedom. At the same time there is also an abundance of things that are not very desirable: struggle, unhappiness, pain.

Scarcity is a game with certain unspoken rules. If we do not know the rules, we will be like the people who refused to see that the emperor's new clothes were fake. Later in the story, a young naïve boy spoke the truth and broke the spell – only then could the true absurdity of the situation be seen. The basic rule of the scarcity game is that you must strive to win at all costs. The flip side of this rule is that losing is always bad and you must do your utmost to avoid it.

Scarcity = Winning at All Costs

A lion was chasing a chamois along a valley. Just when it seemed that the chamois had no possibility of escape, since its path was blocked by a deep ravine, the nimble chamois gathered all its strength and made an heroic leap across the chasm. As it landed safely on the other side, it turned to face the lion. At that moment a fox appeared by the side of the lion and said, 'What with your strength and agility, is it possible that you are going to yield to a feeble chamois? Why do you not gather up your will and make the leap? If you are in earnest you will surely clear the chasm.' At those words the lion's blood began to boil and he gathered all his strength to make the leap. He bounded powerfully towards the ravine and leapt but did not make it and tumbled to his death. Slowly, the fox made its way to the ravine floor to pay the lion its last respects. Over the next few weeks the sly fox set about picking the lion's bones clean.

In her amazingly insightful book, *The Soul of Money* (W. W. Norton & Co. Ltd, 2003), Lynne Twist describes the three toxic myths of scarcity. These are: there is not enough; more is better; and, that is just the way it is. These three assumptions about life lie at the core of the scarcity game. They weave together in an unholy alliance to create the scarcity paradigm.

Scarcity works from a very narrow definition of what life is all about. Scarcity believes that human beings are always in the pursuit of self-interest. Scarcity is founded on the principle that there will always be winners and losers. Winning is naturally good because winners get to do and have lots of things: high salaries; nice homes in the best areas; drive flashy cars; eat in expensive restaurants; travel to exotic places; and secure their children's future by sending them to the best schools. Winners rise up to the top of the pyramid and watch as the losers spiral down. Losing is bad because losers can have a very poor lifestyle. Some losers sleep in the gutter and live through begging while others cannot even afford to keep body and soul together.

The billionaire Warren Buffett is one of the super rich. He has a simple set of rules for making money. Rule number one – never lose money. Rule number two – never forget rule number one. (He was in the news in June 2006 when he made the commitment to give away 85% of his fortune, most of which going to the Bill and Melinda Gates Foundation.)

Because winning is perceived as good and losing as bad, people have been prepared to go to extreme lengths in order to get what they want. Scarcity has a long-standing and bloody relationship with violence and bloodshed. From primitive societies to the military-industrial complexes of our present time, warfare has been the tried and tested way of grabbing other people's resources. In this game there are no prizes for the runner up.

Being wealthy does not necessarily end the scarcity game. Over the years I have known people who have been very wealthy. Having lots of money did not stop them from being caught up in all kinds of worry and unhappiness. A millionaire can feel just as poor on the inside as anyone working hard to make ends meet. One wealthy man whom I know has money, houses and boats coming out of his ears but, when it comes to love and relationships, he is poorer than almost any person I know.

Scarcity is not the same as poverty. A person can live in poverty yet still lead a happy and fulfilled life. A person with a scarcity mindset may have great wealth yet lead an unhappy and unfulfilled life. Scarcity is as much to do with feeling poor on the inside as it is on the outside.

It is a strange twist of the scarcity game that even the top winners end up being losers. In Hollywood, a marriage is as much a business arrangement as an affair of the heart. Around 60% end up in divorce and this has created a whole industry of lawyers, specialist consultants, and therapists – which is hardly surprising considering the huge amounts involved. For instance, Steven Spielberg's divorce cost him over $70 million and Neil Diamond's £100 million. When a Hollywood union goes downhill everyone loses except the divorce lawyers.[6]

There is an old joke about two guys in a jungle who suddenly come across a mean-looking lion. One guy carefully reaches into his knapsack and slowly takes out a set of running shoes and, keeping one eye on the lion, puts them on. The second guy says, 'What are you doing? You can't outrun the lion.' The first guy replies, 'No, but all I have to do is outrun you!'

The fear of losing keeps us motivated to keep our heads above water and play the game. Yet the system is deliberately created in such a way that many will lose. Banks loan money to stimulate business; not everyone will be able to repay those loans and some will default and go bankrupt. That is the way the system is set up. Not everyone can succeed in the marketplace. Some products and services will do well while others will not. There are other ways to lose.

The United Nations Development Programme defines poverty as an inability to live a long, healthy and creative life, to be knowledgeable, or to enjoy a decent standard of living, or self-respect. In the U.S., an estimated 37 million live below the poverty line and around 46 million Americans are without health insurance.[7] In the UK things are not much better. Oxfam estimates that around a quarter of Britain's population lives below the national poverty line and that three million households are in debt to door-to-door money lenders.[8]

The World Bank defines extreme poverty as living on less than $1 per day, and poverty as living on less than $3 per day. As of 2001, 1.1 billion people were living in extreme poverty, and more than 50% were living in poverty. It is estimated that about 8 million people die each year because they are too poor to survive.[9] The charity Oxfam estimates that each year more than 30 million people flee their homes as a result of war, riots, political unrest, floods, earthquakes, volcanoes, typhoons and other forms of conflict and natural disaster. They estimate that over 500,000 people each year are killed in war and that many more have their lives destroyed and their families broken up.[10]

Scarcity thinking leads to suffering and misery. It has led to a crisis of depleted resources, pollution, and industrialization. Scarcity thinking is mindless and wasteful. We buy more stuff and throw it away faster than at any point in our history. Mobile phones are considered out of date after six to nine months. Once we would buy a television and call in the repair man if something were to go wrong. Now it is easier to throw it away and buy a new one. It is not just electrical goods that we throw away. The amount of plastic waste generated annually in the UK is estimated to be nearly 3 million tonnes. An estimated 56% of all plastic waste is used packaging, three-quarters of which is from households. In the UK we consume around 2 billion litres of spring water a year, and most of the empty bottles end up in landfill sites where they take centuries to disintegrate. Over 9 billion plastic bottles are thrown away in the UK each year.[11] Plastic is produced using potentially harmful chemicals, many of which have not undergone environmental risk assessment, and therefore their long term impact on human health and the environment is currently uncertain. Most plastics are non-degradable, which means that they take a long time to break down in landfill sites; no-one knows for certain how long it takes as plastics haven't been around for very long.

Human activities across the planet are having an impact on global climate. The link between global warming and global dimming is no longer hypothetical – carbon dioxide and other greenhouse gases are adversely affecting the planet. Current levels of carbon dioxide are higher than at any time in the past 650,000 years. The northern hemisphere is warmer than it has been for 1,200 years. 2005 was a record year for tropical storms. Hurricane Mitch took 10,000 lives and was the worst storm for 200 years while Hurricane Katrina crippled the oil industry in the Bay of Mexico for a time as well as smashing through New Orleans and the surrounding area. According to insurance claims, in 1995 the global cost of weather-related disasters was around $14 billion. By 2005, it was around $50 billion and rising.[12]

Global pollution is another side-effect of the scarcity mindset. In the rush to get more, we are polluting the earth. For instance, the River Ganges is considered holy by the Hindu people of India. They believe it to be a goddess, and that the river can heal all the sins of people who bathe in its waters. Thousands bathe in its waters each day. Many people are cremated and then thrown into the river which is said to provide a path to heaven. Pollution of the Ganges is now so serious that bathing or drinking the water is very dangerous. Nearly 1 billion litres of largely untreated raw sewage enters the river every day. This, plus the pollution from local industries and the poor control over cremation procedures, results in the river's being a terrible carrier of disease and death.[13]

Changing Your World

The scarcity game is not about individuals: it is about a mass consciousness that manifests through a system. This system will defend its right to survive no matter what. It is not about capitalism or communism: it is about a kind of thinking that will infiltrate and then warp any system.

Capitalism could well become a tremendous force for prosperity on the planet if it could be reformed and its narrow focus on profit widened. Communism could have become a force for prosperity if it could have found the way to truly uniting people to work for the common good.

The prosperity game is not about creating a few thousand more billionaires in the world and hoping that the vibe of prosperity will ripple out and somehow motivate the masses. This has been tried before; it created a fragmented society. Prosperity is not a case of 'my' happiness and wealth at the expense of others or the planet. It is not about 'looking out for number one' or buying more stuff just to prove that we are 'worth it'. True prosperity involves no denial of the self or a sacrifice of one's needs and desires. True prosperity is the possibility of living a life with sufficient money and material things and feeling inwardly fulfilled, happy and on track in life. It is both a journey and an ongoing conversation that involves aliveness, joy and wonder. It is about being happy and achieving meaningful results in the world.

According to John Gall, author of *The Systems Bible* (General Systemantics Press, 2003), systems generally work poorly or not at all; complicated systems seldom exceed five percent efficiency; in complex systems, malfunction and even total non-function can be hard to detect; systems tend to grow, and encroach upon other systems; as they grow in complexity, colossal systems foster colossal errors. He said that we should choose our systems with care.

Real prosperity comes from a system that cares for the whole as well as the individual. Since such a system has not yet been devised, we can only work on changing our consciousness so that we can help to birth a different system on the planet. It is my belief that when enough people embrace prosperity in themselves then the world will change to reflect that shift in consciousness. Prosperity is the revolution that will change the way we live together on the earth. We change the consciousness of scarcity on the planet by addressing scarcity in ourselves. We cannot do this work for another. Yet, unless we change, our world will not. The scarcity game ends when enough people say 'enough is enough'. It will not end when the government or company says it will: it ends when we say it will.

Journal Work ~ A Different World is Possible

What do you most like about the world?

What do you most dislike about the world?

Are you concerned about the state of the world that you are leaving for future generations?

If you were made president of the world for a year, what changes would you make? What would your priorities be – global health, peace, or perhaps trade?

What kind of world do you want to see in the next year? five years? twenty years?

Do not censor any thoughts or emotions.

There are a number of exercises throughout this book. Please record your responses to these in your journal. Please also write down any insights, thoughts, feelings, or questions to the material in this book therein.

References

1. http://www.spartacus.schoolnet.co.uk/FWWcosts.htm
2. http://www.brook.edu/fp/projects/nucwcost/silverberg.htm
3. http://news.bbc.co.uk/1/hi/uk_politics/4804144.stm
4. Boyle, David. *The Little Money Book*. Alistair Sawday Publishing, 2003
5. Boyle, David. *The Little Money Book*. Alistair Sawday Publishing, 2003
6. http://www.screenselect.co.uk/visitor/editorial/824.html
7. http://www.demos.org/pubs/KitchenTable016.pdf
8. http://www.oxfamgb.org/ukpp/poverty/thefacts.htm
9. http://www.unmillenniumproject.org/documents/
    TimeMagazineMar142005-TheEndofPovertysmall1.pdf
10. http://www.oxfam.org.uk/what_we_do/issues/conflict_disasters/index.htm
11. http://www.wasteonline.org.uk/resources/InformationSheets/Plastics.htm
12. http://edition.cnn.com/2005/WEATHER/12/19/hurricane.season.ender/
    index.html
13. http://en.wikipedia.org/wiki/Ganga_Pollution

Part Two

Prosperity = The Way of Heart and Mind

Chapter 4

Prosperity = Changing the Game

A journey of a thousand miles begins with a single step.
LAO TZU

There is an old story about a small boy who banged a drum all day and loved every moment of it. He would not be quiet, no matter what anyone else said or did and various people were called in by neighbours and asked to do something about the child. The first told the boy that he would, if he continued to make so much noise, damage his eardrums; but this reasoning was too advanced for the child, who was neither a scientist nor a scholar. The second told him that drum beating was a sacred activity and should be carried out only on special occasions. The third offered the neighbours plugs for their ears; the fourth gave the boy a book; the fifth gave the neighbours books that described a method of controlling their anger; and the sixth gave the boy meditation exercises to make him placid and explained that all reality was imagination. Each of these remedies worked for a short while, but none worked for very long. Eventually, a real master came along. He looked at the situation, handed the boy a hammer and chisel, and said, 'I wonder what is inside the drum?'

Principle Four	*We change our game by looking at what binds us to scarcity. We free ourselves from scarcity by the degree to which we face and feel our core fears, resistance and pain.*

Prosperity = Opening to Change

The scarcity game is endemic and many are thoroughly sick of it. Some have found a way to play differently. Some recognize the game for what it is and would leave it if only they knew how. Most are not even aware that they are playing the game.

Prosperity does not arise through ignoring scarcity, nor does it come about just by thinking happy thoughts. If we were sitting on a hot stove we would instantly jump off. We would not give it a second thought. Scarcity is more like the boiled frog syndrome where the water is heated so gradually that we do not notice we are being boiled alive.

True prosperity is about inner and outer richness. We are not really prosperous if we are wealthy on the outside but feel poor on the inside. The same holds true if we feel wealthy on the inside but are not able to manifest an abundant world on the outside.

True prosperity is about feeling wealthy, where our real and very present physical needs and desires can be fulfilled. It is also about living a life that includes emotional richness. Prosperity is about having access to a rich world of beliefs and ideas and being able to think wealthy thoughts, not just occasionally, but all the time. Prosperity is about living in a world that has an abundance of life force energy and spirit. Prosperity is about creating another world, one of possibility for ourselves, our loved ones and our descendants.

As a race, we are naturally creative and inventive, not aggressive and greedy. Prosperity is the natural state of the natural world. Nature is totally abundant; one sunflower, for instance, will produce thousands of seeds. The sun produces enough energy for our needs many times over; we have not worked out how to harness it fully yet. If we were to give prosperity a chance, it would create a different world.

For anyone living in the herd mentality of the scarcity game, prosperity is like believing in the Land of Oz or Shangri-la – an enticing yet imaginary place. The prosperity game is real; there are people already playing it. If you feel immersed in the scarcity game, do not worry. The majority of us are born into it and we need to find our own way out. We need to change the way we play the game.

The *I Ching,* also known as *The Book of Changes,* states that everything changes all of the time. As the Buddha said, 'everything is impermanent'. Change is a natural part of life. Prosperity is about embracing change and also about dealing with our resistance to change. Change is about exchanging one mindset (one set of behaviours and experiences) for another. Tony Buzan, the co-founder of Mind Maps, makes in his book *Embracing Change* (BBC Books, 2005) the distinction between natural and enforced change. Natural change is something which we accept, anticipate, embrace, plan, and manage. As a means of exiting the scarcity game, natural change works very well. Enforced change is an imposition, something that is unexpectedly thrust upon us; whether we are ready for it or not, we are catapulted into something unfamiliar. Enforced change happens when we are a little stubbornly attached to the old game, meaning that we are stuck in an old routine and not even looking up at the rock face. When we are stuck in dull work, debt, lack of money, confusion, being aimless in life, ongoing dramas, unexpected bills, struggle, or a string of bad luck then enforced change is a gift that will jolt us out of the scarcity game. People who resist natural change will tend to be confronted by enforced change at some point. This is because life itself does not support the scarcity game. Within the prosperity game itself there is an intelligence that seeks to nudge us elsewhere, but more about that later.

A few years back I met someone who had undergone a period of enforced change. He was a high flyer in the city and spent several years building a new and highly successful business. Although his real passion was for art he never had much time to devote to it. He poured all of his time and energy into his work until eventually he burnt out and fell ill. He had ignored the warning signs and had sailed past the point of no return. He left the City a rich man some years later, yet his health is still very poor and he has to shield himself from even small amounts of stress in his life.

Tom worked in the media industry in the U.S. During an illness that lasted a year, he was able to reflect on his life and often went to art galleries to sit and lift his spirits. It slowly dawned on him that this was the opportunity to change his life. He always wanted to be an artist and, despite having no formal art training, he made the leap of faith. He now has a studio, and says that art saved his life.

The Chinese pictogram for 'crisis' is composed of the characters meaning 'opportunity' and 'danger'. When we ignore the warning signs in life we are heading for danger. The Titanic sunk on her maiden voyage from Southampton to New York City because many warnings were ignored. The ship had received several warnings on the day she sunk; six were ignored and one never made it to the bridge.

Effective Change = Small Steps

There are three principles to bear in mind about effective change:

1. Small changes are easier to commit to than massive leaps;

2. Small changes are easier to instigate and integrate;

3. Small changes add up to incredible change over time.

Prosperity = Acknowledging Our Resistance to Change

The journey from scarcity to prosperity is challenging because it requires us to confront what is not working in our lives. This means facing inner discomfort and pain. It is unavoidable. Nothing stops us from being prosperous as powerfully as we ourselves do. We have our foot on the brake pedal and wonder why nothing much is happening in our lives. We might call this our unconscious resistance to being prosperous.

Resistance could also be called self-blocking, self-delaying tactics, self-sabotage or self-undermining. Sometimes resistance seems to come from other people. No amount of external resistance has any power to stop us if there is an absence of internal resistance. When there is a strong internal resistance to something then even a little external resistance can seem like a strong block.

Making resistance conscious is the first step in the prosperity game. This is challenging because resistance cannot be seen, touched, heard, or smelled. However, resistance can be felt and it certainly does have consequences.

One woman was upset that her husband left her for another woman. She took a couple of years doing personal development workshops to help her work through her anger. At a certain point she felt able to move on. She began to date other men and generally allow more fun into her life. However, she could not openly show her happiness because she was worried that her estranged husband would find out and stop supporting her financially. She felt that he was more likely to continue giving her money if she seemed miserable.

Resistance happens when different parts of us want different things. We may want freedom and yet crave safety, we may desire adventure yet fear disappointment. Resistance can come as a result of a conflict between a duty and a dream. Resistance feels like a push-pull game of moving in one direction and simultaneously pulling in another direction.

Resistance is an internal process which both protects us and prevents change from happening. It is rather like a suit of armour which we put on to go into battle but then forget to take off for the ball. Then we wonder why few people want to dance with us.

Have you ever decided to do something and then not done it? Have you ever thought about practising meditation, or doing martial arts or starting jogging or a language class and never got around to it? Welcome to the world of resistance.

Resistance is ubiquitous in the Western world. Resistance can slow us down or speed us up. Resistance wants to help us avoid feeling bad about ourselves. Underlying this is an attempt not to feel pain; we have been taught that pain is bad. Very few people have been taught to face and feel their pain. We resist many things in life, including prosperity, because we want to protect ourselves from pain. There are many kinds of resistance that keep us playing small in life. Here are a few to stimulate your inquiry.

1. **(Over) Achieving:** The tendency towards achievement is no bad thing in itself: it becomes resistance when we become fixated on a goal and forget that life is a journey. Over-achieving is like living life as a tick-box list of things to achieve, experience or accumulate. This kind of achieving results in plenty of doing and very little being. This tendency drives the rat race and leads to achieving at any cost, which usually ends in burn out.

    Antidote: stillness and silence; more being and less doing.

2. **Feeling anxious:** This is the tendency to dwell on problems and worst case scenarios. Not only is this depressing and a cause for concern but it blocks any real feeling for what is actually going on in a situation. It is possible to worry about many things in the scarcity game. We can worry about worrying too much. This type of thinking is a kind of loop with no seeming way out. After a while, it adversely impacts on our confidence, health and self-esteem.

    Antidote: embrace courage and take small daily risks.

3. **Seeking approval:** This is the tendency towards constantly needing the approval of others, which prevents free thought and action. It creates a behaviour concerned with pleasing, which is dependent upon what others think. Here, actions are taken out of a need to be liked. This leads to conformity, where we behave, dress, think, and speak, according to other people's standards or values. We feel afraid of straying too far from the herd; conformists believe in safety in numbers.

    Antidote: seek to know your own truth and authenticity; understand and fulfill your own needs.

4. **Being too busy:** This is the tendency to fill up the day with things to do. There is always a checklist of things that need doing and never enough time to do them. Busyness leaves no space for change. The scarcity game is filled with people rushing about doing all manner of things except really living. Busyness is an avoidance of real living. It is a habit that squeezes the joy from life. At the core of busyness is the belief that people only love us for what we do rather than for who we are.

Antidote: more being and less doing; embrace the possibility that you are loveable for being who you are.

5.   **Clinging:** This is a tendency to hold on to the past no matter how painful or difficult it is. We seek resolution by clinging, which never works. People often confuse holding on with love. Clinging is a childlike reaction and a kind of malingering. As children, we may clutch mother's skirt when we are afraid; as adults, it is a rather poor strategy. Clinging is an avoidance of the present moment.

Antidote: let go on all levels; be in the present; look to taking the next step in your life.

6.   **Making comparisons:** This is a tendency to make value judgements in terms of good and bad, right and wrong. We may compare our behaviour, achievements, relationships, status, dress sense, earnings… the list is endless. This produces a feeling of being better or worse off than other people. It fuels the 'keeping up with the Joneses' mentality. Comparison fuels feelings of envy and jealousy and thoughts that life is unfair.

Antidote: focus on your positive strengths and qualities, bless the strengths and qualities that you see in others.

7.   **Being complacent:** This tendency is based on the belief that success or failure continue or go away on their own. The attitude of complacency has no sense of responsibility and no urgency to act. Being complacent means that we do not really see reality. It is a killer and many an individual or company has slipped under as a result.

Antidote: start creating some juicy goals, take some positive actions; believe that what you think and do counts.

8.   **Complaining:** This is a tendency to get our needs met through pointing out mistakes and problems. By complaining we seek to gain compensation. It tends to drain vital energy from the person doing it and also from the people hearing it. Scarcity rewards the loudest or the weakest. Complaining is painful. It keeps us stuck, thinking about the things which we do not like.

Antidote: focus on what you want, rather than on what you do not want; appreciate all your blessings.

9.   **Controlling:** Control manifests internally and externally. Internal control is concerned with repression of thoughts and feelings. External control is concerned with rules and regulations for how

other people should behave. Control freaks cannot bear disorder or chaos of any kind; it threatens their need for stability. Needing to be in control is a painful aspect of perfectionism.

Antidote: practise being in the flow; release the word 'should' from your vocabulary; trust yourself; give yourself and others some space.

10. Focusing on disappointment: This is dwelling on all the mistakes, pain or traumas of the past. Disappointment is a resistance to feeling pain, or heart-break. Whenever we have felt our heart broken by what other people did or did not do, we resist moving forward out of fear of its happening again.

   Antidote: have compassion for yourself; take heart that the future can always be different from the past.

11. Feeling guilty: This is the tendency to feel bad on account of what has happened in the past. Sometimes, guilt arises for no apparent reason other than the feeling of being guilty just for being alive. Guilt offers no solutions to past mistakes and is a form of self-punishment. Guilt prevents real change from happening. Guilt keeps people locked into feeling valueless.

   Antidote: stop blaming yourself; acknowledge your mistakes, correct them, learn from them and move on.

12. Identifying with a role: In the scarcity game we can go into what the spiritual teacher Ram Dass calls 'somebody training' where we start to live an illusion of who we think we should be. We become a persona, a mask, a shell, and we lose touch with the centre of our naturalness and become locked into a role – such as a boss, a mother, a worker, a student, a coach, a high-flyer, a helpful person, or a drop-out. Identifying with a role means that we are not being our authentic selves.

   Antidote: realize that no role defines who you really are; know you are not special in any way but that you are unique in every way.

13. Becoming a martyr: This is the tendency to feel burdened, self-righteous and unappreciated. People with an attitude of martyrdom seldom complain about their workload although they may secretly feel very angry and self-pitying. Martyrdom is about suffering, pure and simple. Martyrs believe that sacrifice is always noble, that it is right to work hard and wrong to enjoy life too much. Martyrs are good at punishing themselves and others.

Antidote: be less dour about life; lighten up and let your hair down; allow in more fun and laughter.

14. **Struggling for power:** This is the tendency to fight our corner and for what we believe is right. The underlying fear is that other people will dominate and we will lose if we do not fight. People get into power struggles over money, obligation, roles, sex, time, agreements and property. Competition is a form of power struggle where winning is thought to equal happiness. What we resist persists.

    Antidote: choose being happy over the need to be right.

15. **Procrastinating:** This is the tendency to put things off for another day. It can result from being overloaded with too many choices, all of them equally difficult or unattractive. It is about having no clear sense of direction or no real feeling of passion for anything. It can occur as a result of experiencing too much stick and not enough carrot in life.

    Antidote: find the little things in life you feel passionate about; do something you want to do (anything!) and then keep on doing it.

16. **Feeling resentful:** This is the tendency to feel that we are forced into doing things, and feeling that we have little or no choice in the matter. Behind resentment is hidden anger that resists moving forward. Resentment arises out of a pre-occupation with what others have done, are doing or are not doing. Resentment is a very powerful scarcity pattern.

    Antidote: accept and bless people and things just the way they are; bless the things you resent; see that they are perfect just the way they are.

17. **Being self-critical:** The scarcity game is fiercely critical: it is not pleasant. This creates an inner critic who speaks to us 24/7 about what is wrong with us. This is the tendency to put ourselves down with vicious force. It is a defence mechanism that seeks to pre-empt other people's put-downs. The idea is that, if we get in first, it will not hurt so much. Being self-critical is lethal.

    Antidote: be gentle on yourself; find ways to nurture, love, and accept yourself.

18. **Doubting ourselves:** This is the tendency to create limiting thoughts around why things always go badly for us, why people should not be trusted and ultimately why we cannot be trusted. Self-doubt leads to

a scattering of our energy and to non-action. Self-doubt is the great destroyer of faith, trust and self-belief. Self-doubt stops any new project or venture in its tracks. Self-doubt is usually present whenever a bold step into the unknown is being considered.

Antidote: trust yourself; learn from your mistakes and your successes; take small achievable steps that build your sense of trust.

19. Sabotaging ourselves: Self-sabotage can come in the form of accidents, drama and incidents. This one is subtle because it can seem that external forces are at work rather than internal self-sabotage. Self-sabotage creates the feeling of being unlucky and flirting with disaster. This is the tendency to trip ourselves up in order to stop any forward movement. Things just happen. Sabotaging ourselves is a way to avoid moving forward into greater levels of success. Self-sabotage is a form of self-punishment. Self-punishment is a belief that we do not deserve to succeed and we deserve to suffer instead.

Antidote: slow down; examine your desires and outcomes, be aware of any conflicting desires, get clear on what you really want; know you deserve to succeed.

20. Feeling shame: This is a fundamental feeling of being flawed and defective, of feeling bad and dirty, of feeling undeserving to be alive. Shame can come from a core sense of abandonment. People who feel deep shame may seek approval and have a disabled sense of autonomy. People who have been shamed may adopt addictive or compulsive behaviour to escape from the core pain of shame. Shame is painful; it is a great destroyer of personal aspirations and dreams.

Antidote: stop taking responsibility for things that are not your fault; acknowledge your shame and embrace your own natural state of innocence: you have a right to be here on the earth.

21. Being a victim: This is a feeling of being weak and helpless in the face of reality. It is a dependent way of living, based on subtle blackmail and emotional manipulation. Victims present themselves as a burden to other people. They create drama and trauma for themselves. Victims are trapped in a pattern that stops them from feeling able to take personal responsibility for their lives.

Antidote: start to take more personal responsibility; know you have all the resources to deal with the challenges that life brings your way.

Prosperity = Beyond Resistance to Facing Fear

Another word for resistance is fear. Beneath every resistance is some form of fear; it is the glue that keeps us stuck in the scarcity game. Fear is the deepest level of our resistance to prosperity. The author Susan Jeffers spoke about dealing with fear in her groundbreaking book, *Feel the Fear and Do It Anyway* (Rider & Co. 1997). According to Jeffers, beneath all our fears is the core idea that we can't handle whatever life brings us; we feel fear because we think that we cannot handle things like humiliation, vulnerability, getting old, or losing our home and all our money. We can be afraid of almost anything – we may feel afraid of expressing intimacy, of being playful and joyous, even of speaking too loudly or laughing too much. Fear has many aspects, some fears are irrational, some unpredictable. We may fear being alone, going broke, changing career, ending or beginning a relationship, being interviewed, speaking in public, failure, disapproval, or rejection. Although many people are afraid of failure, many more are afraid of being successful.

A therapist friend of mine told me a story about a very unhappy client. He asked her if she could remember a time when she had no problems. She answered, 'Yes, a few years ago I had no problems for a couple of weeks.' My friend asked her what had happened then. She replied, 'I couldn't handle it!'

According to research,[1] the fear of public speaking is stronger than the fear of death itself. This seems strange, but then fear is not always rational. Similarly, our fears around money are often irrational. We may fear losing money, or having it taken away from us. We may fear that we are not confident, smart or good enough to earn much of it. Fear does not go away: it is our companion on the journey from scarcity to prosperity.

The more we face our fear, the less power over us it has. The more we avoid it, the stronger it grows. Fear is not something bad to be avoided. Freedom comes from befriending fear and making it an ally. Fear is very useful when it warns us against doing something foolhardy. However, when it is not connected to reality but exists in the form of fearful imaginings that go on in our heads, it is a blocking energy. In this case, it often takes the form of, 'well, this is what happened in the past so it will probably happen in my future'. This kind of fear becomes a powerful enemy. Fear becomes a friend when we learn to welcome it and transform it into something useful. For instance, all good actors know how to channel nervous energy into their performance. Some of the best actors, including Sir Laurence Olivier, learned to use fear to improve the impact of their performance. If you have ever engaged in an activity such as abseiling, hand gliding or mountaineering, then you will have found that fear and excitement are feelings which are very close to each other. The energy of excitement is merely fear combined with the expectation of a positive outcome. In the scarcity game, fear is something to be ashamed of: in the prosperity game, it is something to be honoured and made use of.

Several years ago I attended a workshop about money and, during one of the breaks, I started a conversation with one of the participants. I sensed this young woman's underlying nervousness and I wondered how she was doing. She soon shared her story. She was a social worker and felt passionate about social justice. Several months previously, the unthinkable happened – a distant relative had died leaving her a considerable amount of money. She had become a millionaire and, at the same time, a prisoner of her wealth. She was so distraught that she had booked a place on the money workshop to help her discover what to do. Just as the tea break came to an end, she confessed that she was considering just giving the money away. I only just managed to restrain an impulse to hand her my business card!

Facing Fear

What is your greatest fear?

What is your specific fear of failure in the work that you do?
What is your specific fear of success in the work that you do?

If you were to lose all of your money, what do you fear would happen to you?
If you were to win many millions tomorrow, what do you fear would happen?
What fears regarding money do you have for your family or other people?
Do you believe that people would behave differently towards you if you were richer or poorer than you are currently?

What do you stand to lose by not facing your fear now?
Can you imagine your life beyond your fear?

Prosperity = Facing Pain

Beneath all of our resistance lies the core pain that we are desperately trying to avoid. People often seek to avoid feeling pain through a number of distractions, including spending money or working too hard. In the scarcity game, pain is a nuisance which must be switched off by painkillers, alcohol or addictive and distracting behaviour. In the prosperity game, pain is a signal that something is amiss; it tells us that something needs to be addressed. Prosperity tells us to look at the pain: scarcity tells us to get rid of it, to sweep it under the carpet.

When we resist feeling our pain, we create an inner conflict against the pain which we do not want. This results in an inner dynamic of tension. When we accept the pain, however, we end the fight. Fighting keeps the pain locked inside of us. Acceptance is a willingness to see reality as it truly is. Non-acceptance looks at reality and says that it should be different. Acceptance of reality is one of the most powerful ways to dissolve resistance. Pain might last an instant: suffering can last a whole lifetime. Suffering is resistance to feeling pain. The person who truly feels the intensity of their pain begins to unravel it. This, in turn, ends their resistance to life. The person who suppresses or avoids their pain is like a pressure-cooker that will one day explode. The only way out is to expect the pain that the scarcity game brings – whether that pain comes from not being loved enough, not being accepted enough, not being given enough or not being held enough. Unless we face our pain and take responsibility for it, we will pass it on to the next generation.

Pain is a signpost pointing towards the prosperity game. The gateway is narrow and challenging and not many wish to pass through. If we resist pain it will become suffering, which is the game play of scarcity. The good news is that facing and feeling our pain and resistance is the way to transform it. We can end the suffering of a lifetime by facing our pain for a few days or hours.

The Antidote of Acceptance

What do you find most difficult to accept in the world?
What things or people in your life do you find difficult to accept?
What do you find most difficult to accept in yourself?
Can you find some compassion and acceptance for your pain?

Prosperity = The Possibility of Freedom

Freedom is a path that takes courage. It is something that we must desire above all else. When we are truly free, money and possessions cannot trap us. Too many people seek freedom through the accumulation of more money. The trick is to find what gives us a sense of freedom first and then allow money to open up the way for that freedom to come in the outside world. We cannot buy freedom, but if we feel free then money can open the way to even greater freedom. Many people have pointed the way to freedom.

When Martin Luther King Jr stood to speak at a rally in 1963, near the Lincoln Memorial in Washington, he had originally prepared a short and formal speech about the sufferings of African Americans attempting to realize their freedom in a society chained by discrimination. He finished speaking and was about to sit down when gospel singer Mahalia Jackson called out, 'Tell them about your dream, Martin! Tell them about the dream!' Encouraged by shouts from the audience, King continued to speak and the result became the landmark statement of civil rights in America – a dream of all people, of all races and colours and backgrounds, sharing in an America marked by freedom and democracy. The next year he was awarded the Nobel Peace Prize.

Pablo Picasso was an artist who chose to pursue his art even though he had scant financial means of support. He had little formal education and was for a long time quite poor. When he moved to a studio in Barcelona, he did not have the money to furnish it properly and so amused himself by painting the missing pieces of furniture on the walls. Picasso ended up a rich man – not only because he died a wealthy man but because he did not allow a lack of money early on in life to stop him following his heart. He pursued his heart and his art and it made him a wealthy man.

We cannot know the end results of our labours: we can but take one step at a time. This journey is a little scary, unsteady and uncertain at first, but in time compelling and often liberating. The way is uncertain at the beginning since the path must be discovered. In the early stages of the transition from scarcity to prosperity there is a need for slow perseverance, for a gentle pace, and for awareness. This is not the time for rushing headlong and losing sight of the journey by chasing some dream or vision. If we are going too quickly, we might make an error of judgement.

There is a story about a man hitting gold during the gold rush in California but lacking the essential equipment to keep going so he returned home to borrow money from friends and relatives to buy the necessary mining equipment to keep going. The initial returns were good but suddenly the gold run out. He kept digging but there was no more gold. Eventually, he gave up and sold the equipment to a junkman. The junkman was no fool and he called in an engineer to survey the mine. The engineer reported that it was likely that the prospector had hit a fault in the vein. This meant that the vein of gold probably continued just a few feet away. The junkman invested in the mine and, sure enough, struck the vein again just three feet on and made a fortune. Within us all awaits a rich vein of untapped potential; some people never dig for it or start digging in the wrong place. Others dig in the right place and then give up too soon. Prosperity is a journey of a thousand miles that begins with the first step.

At the beginning, the way is not clear, we cannot always see the path and our vision is limited. When we begin to change the game in ourselves, it is important to take baby steps so that vital energy is conserved for the journey. People fall by the wayside because they are confronted by the inevitable challenge, the unavoidable obstacle, and do not have enough energy for the task. Peter had his own business in Milan, Italy where he organized medical seminars around the world for doctors and other specialists. The job often involved long hours and could get very stressful. It was a complex business and keeping tabs on the cash flow was a continual problem. Finally, the business was declared bankrupt. He moved to London and applied to live in a community in central London. On his application, he put down that he was a 'soup therapist.' Intrigued, the community invited him along to join them. He now has less money but more time and less stress. He also has more friendships and more time to follow his passion of playing music. For Peter, the journey is still in the early stages. At times he misses his native homeland and he is still uncertain about his direction. He takes one day at a time.

The reward for facing our fear is greater freedom. Family therapist Virginia Satir says that there are five freedoms: the freedom to see and hear what is, instead of what should be, was, or will be; the freedom to say what you feel and think, instead of what you should; the freedom to feel what you actually feel, instead of what you ought; the freedom to ask for what you want, instead of always waiting for permission; and the freedom to take risks on your own behalf, instead of choosing to be only 'secure' and not rocking the boat.

Freedom Review

Note down several areas of your life that are important to you – such as health, leisure, relationships, family, personal growth, money and work.

On a scale of 1 to 10, how much freedom do you experience in each area?

If you were more free in these areas, how different would your life feel?

The Ability to Change = Freedom

Research has shown that the best way to induce change is to make it a discipline for 30 days to break the usual routine and just to do something else.

For the next 30 days, choose one area of your life in which to do something different each day. Then, every day, do one thing differently. If you choose relationships, speak to a stranger or consciously smile to one every day for the next 30 days. If you are more daring, you could flirt a little with a stranger everyday.

If you choose health, eat something very different every day. If you choose work, take a different route to work each day. If you choose money, give a little money away each day to someone homeless or buy yourself a small treat everyday.

Just Imagine...

Imagine that you decide not to change. How would your life look life in 5 years, 10 years, and 20 years? Wind your life forward to its end point; you are just about to cross the way between this world and the next. How do you want to have lived your life?

What accomplishments have you achieved? How much love, joy, happiness and laughter have you experienced? How much difference has your life made to others?

What would you choose – a life of boredom, bitterness and regret or a well-lived life which brings riches beyond measure?

References

1. http://www.lindacrabtree.com/cmtnews/Stress/ The 14 worst fears.htm

Chapter 5

Prosperity = Truly Growing Up

It is better to follow your own life mission, however imperfectly, than to assume the life mission of another person, however successfully.

BHAGAVAD GITA

There was an old sow with three little piglets; she was so poor that she could not keep them, so sadly she sent them out to seek their fortune. On the road, the first and youngest little pig met a man with a bundle of straw. The little pig persuaded the man to hand over the straw and the little pig built a house with it. Then along came a wolf, and knocked at the door asking to come in. The little pig refused and the wolf blew the house down and ate up the little pig. The second and next youngest little pig met a man with a bundle of sticks, and persuaded the man to give him the sticks to build a house with them. Then along came a wolf and he knocked at the door, asking to come in. The little pig refused and the wolf blew the house down and ate up the little pig. The third little pig, that was the eldest and wisest, met a man with a cart of bricks, and persuaded him to give him the bricks to build a house with them. Then, sure enough, along came the wolf and, seeing the house, he strode right up and knocked at the door... .

Principle Five   *Prosperity is the state of being an authentic adult. We become an authentic adult by acknowledging and honouring our core needs, boundaries and values.*

Prosperity = Embracing Our Needs

The story of the three little pigs is a metaphor for three stages of human development. Psychologists say that the maturation process from childhood to adulthood relates to moving from dependency to independence. The first little pig is the most naive and builds a flimsy house of straw that has little power to resist the wolf. The second little pig is a little wiser and builds a sturdier house but still it is not strong enough to resist the wolf. The third little pig not only builds a solid house that the wolf could not blow down but is able to predict the behaviour of the wolf and so avoid being eaten.

We each of us have these three aspects within us. The first is the dependent state. We enter the world as vulnerable children and are dependent upon those around us to take care of our needs. All human beings have needs and this is nothing to be ashamed of. We need shelter, feeding, love, intimacy and touch. We need connection with our caretakers in order to understand ourselves as we are growing up. Children who grow up not feeling ashamed of any aspect of themselves (their bodies, emotions, or forming intellects) will become naturally playful, open, joyful, happy, bold, adventurous, and full of wonder. When a child's core needs are met, he or she is able to move to the next stage of development, that of independence. Not everyone makes it and many adults are stuck in dependency mode. In the scarcity game, children rarely receive the love and care that they would like. Children are vulnerable and open to the environment in which they find themselves. Some parents have never really had their own needs met and so do not know how to meet the needs of their children. Some children are forced to be silent and to squash their inquisitive nature. Children who are not allowed to be themselves will seek approval, attention and love in any way they can. They stop being themselves and become adaptive to their circumstances.

Being stuck in a childlike state leads to a demand that life be a certain way. When life does not deliver then there is the inevitable upset. Dependence is a feeling of being needy, and then acting from a needy place. This results in feeling bad for acting in a needy fashion, which feeds the feeling of being needy. It is a vicious circle of unmet needs.

When a child grows up with a fundamental need that is not met, he or she has been conditioned into scarcity. In many families, qualities such as acceptance, communication, fun, love and understanding are scarce commodities. Children need to experience these not just as concepts or words but as physical, tangible things. Children need things like hugs and smiles and even presents on their birthday. When love is scarce then this unmet need will play out in a number of ways later in life. People seek love through many pseudo symbols such as money, possessions, relationships, or sex. The dependent mindset sees a world of 'not enough' and will grab what it can through inappropriate, dramatic and even self-harming ways. When money equals love, the scramble for money will be a scramble for love. Many high flyers in life not only chase the symbols of success in order to feel better about themselves but use money and possessions to fill the hole inside them where the needy child still lives. When we do not receive enough love as children, no amount of relationships or fast cars will fill the gap. In the end, only love will fill the need for love that was unmet in childhood. Nothing else will do.

People with unmet needs from childhood may feel a degree of isolation, abandonment, and rigidity and may also feel that they are only lovable if someone else loves them first. Some get stuck looking for love all of their lives. Some get caught in abusive and unhappy relationships with other people who are also unresolved and stuck at some level.

For some, dependency is a permanent way of behaving. As adults, there are times when we feel dependent on others – perhaps because of temporary conditions such as pregnancy, illness or accident. Such things naturally make us dependent on others for short periods of time. However, habitual dependency makes us victims of the scarcity game. When we operate from a mindset of habitual dependency, we feel that we cannot cope with what life brings and that we cannot take complete responsibility for ourselves. We then tend to move from disaster to disaster and live in the hope that someone will rescue us. Like a damsel in distress waiting for a white knight. Dependent people are often angry, although in many cases they cannot express that anger and so tend either to turn it upon themselves or to resort to passive aggressive behaviour.

The dependent mindset is that of a victim; we all play victim from time to time. Every time that we blame our childhood, circumstances, politicians, the boss or another nationality, we are playing the victim. This is very disempowering. It allows us to stop being responsible for what we think, say, choose or do. We can then shift the responsibility for what happens to us in our life on to others. The victim mentality is habitual; the more we do it, the more we get stuck in it. Victims do not need help in solving their problems: they need help in discovering that they have all the resources they need to meet their own challenges.

Prosperity is about understanding and honouring our basic needs as a developing human being. We have biological needs (for food, drink, shelter, warmth and sleep); safety needs (for protection, security, order and stability); social needs (to belong to a supportive family or group; to feel wanted, loved and connected to others); achievement and autonomy needs (to move towards meaningful goals, to realize our potential and to have a sense of real purpose). We have needs to laugh, play and celebrate,

to be creative, enjoy beauty and have fun. We also have spiritual needs –
to know our deep, authentic self beyond the confines of the personality,
and to know and connect with a greater universal reality or source.

Understanding Needs

What are your basic needs for security and safety?
What are your basic needs for belonging and relating?
What are your basic needs for celebration and play?
What are your basic needs for self-esteem and achievement?
What are your basic needs for freedom and growth?
What are your basic needs for beauty and harmony?
What are your basic needs for spiritual awakening and growth?

What are your priority needs that are not being met right now?

What needs do you feel ashamed of?

As we grow up, we all need to deal with the internal dilemma of
vulnerability versus power. If we have too much vulnerability, we may
seem weak. Some men, in particular, find being vulnerable difficult. If we
have too much power, we may seem to be cold and hard. Both men and
women can find being powerful difficult. Problems arise when a person
feels ashamed of their vulnerability and seeks to suppress it or cover it up
with a hard exterior. Repressing or hiding vulnerability does not work in
the long run. If we lose touch with our vulnerable side, we lose touch
with our needs and our childlike spontaneity and zest for life. We can
become deadly serious adults. The world of work is filled with such
people and working with them can be a deadly serious affair.

Vulnerability is not generally welcomed in the workplace. A person
who is emotionally upset may be told to pull themselves together or get
a grip. When the world seems like a place of hard knocks, we will feel
vulnerable when dealing with money, and when negotiating with
others, particularly if we feel that people are judging us or are out to
cheat us.

When we lose touch with our vulnerable side, we lose touch with our
core feelings. As we grow up, we learn to communicate in terms of
analysis, planning, thinking and judgements, rather than in terms of
feelings and needs. We are taught to rise above our feelings and keep a
stiff upper lip. Of course, this might be truer of Britain than Brazil.
However, displays of emotion in the workplace do not necessarily mean
that people are expressing their true feelings. Maria worked in a large

publication firm in Northern Italy. Although the culture is emotionally expressive in general, Maria told me that feelings were not encouraged at work and so were expressed in private, such as in chats in corridors. Sometimes, however, feelings would boil over in volcanic outbursts of rage but, even then, it was usually only the boss who was allowed to be angry. Workers rarely felt that they had such permission and tended to express their anger through non-cooperation and subtle forms of sabotage (such as not passing on information) and indulging in office politics.

People generally tend to defend themselves against judgements but feel more open to a communication that is based on real feelings. We tend to hide our vulnerability out of a fear of judgement and shaming. We may feel vulnerable when faced with a new situation. We may feel vulnerable when confronted with a problem which we imagine we do not have the resources to deal with.

We may feel vulnerable when voicing our true feelings with others or when sharing our creative work with the world. In the scarcity game, people hide their feelings and this leads to a lack of clarity and unease in relationships. There is a heavy price to pay for concealing feelings.

People often think that they are communicating a feeling when all they are really doing is thinking and judging. The following statements are diagnoses and judgements rather than feelings even though they begin with the words 'I feel':

'I feel that you should know better.'

'I feel that you do not care about me.'

'I feel that everything I do is useless.'

We are expressing feelings when we say:

'I feel sad about...'

'I feel happy when...'

'I feel angry when...'

People who cannot feel try to feel by thinking. This is impossible. We feel through being in touch with our body and by honouring our feelings. It is a great pity that so many seem unable to feel. We have such a great range of feelings from deep sadness to tremendous joy. The more deeply we are able to feel uncomfortable feelings, such as sadness and hatred, the more highly we can reach for joy and love.

We have feelings because we have needs. It is really hard to separate the two. People who express their needs have a better chance of getting them met. Expressing needs means taking a risk but this must be weighed against the risk of not having them met. People feel alive, cheerful, contented, happy, free, glowing, inspired, moved, relieved, and stimulated when their needs are met. People feel afraid, angry, ashamed, depressed, disappointed, tired, and uncomfortable when they are repressing or not communicating their needs.

Marshal Rosenberg, the founder of Non-Violent Communication, tells the story of his mother who once attended a workshop he was leading. A group of women were discussing how frightening it was to express their needs when suddenly his mother got up, left the room and didn't return for a long time. When she eventually returned she looked very pale. In the presence of the group, Marshal asked her if she was all right. She replied that she had suddenly realized that she was angry with her husband for not having met her needs and that it had just occurred to her that she had never told him what she needed.[1]

If we do not even know what our needs are, we have little hope of communicating them. If we are afraid of communicating our needs, we have little hope of realizing them. We may express our needs and find that other people do not want to comply. Expressing our needs is no guarantee of their fulfilment but until we learn to take a risk and express them appropriately we have little chance of being fulfilled on a deep level.

Dependent adults need to get in touch with their core needs and express them. This is instrumental in moving to the next developmental stage, which is that of the independent adult.

Expressing Feelings and Needs

What needs do you have to belong, to be understood, to be loved? On a scale of 1 to 10, how good are you at expressing your needs?

Practise communicating your needs. Try small things first and then work up to the expression of bigger needs. Start with, 'I really feel the need for a bath / exotic meal / walk...' In time, you can build up to expressing a need for more intimate things, like certain expressions of care and love.

Start to communicate your feelings, rather than your thinking. Notice the language you use. Which communications get you the results you want? Which do not?

Avoid expressing needs or feelings as a way to get other people to do things for you. Have no agenda, other than that of wishing to he in heartfelt communication with another person.

Taking Responsibility

What areas of your life do you feel that you are not responsible for?
Who do you blame for the circumstances of your life?
What failures do you refuse to be responsible for?
What successes do you refuse to be responsible for?

Practise taking responsibility for everything in your life.
Practise taking responsibility for what you say, think and do.

Prosperity = Having Healthy Boundaries

As children, we move from dependence to independence as we mature into adolescence. Moving into independence is about our maturing need for a sense of identity separate from our caretakers. Adolescents are faced with hormonal changes in the body and they must start making choices about who they think they are, and what they stand for. Adulthood is peeking scarily over the horizon and the care-free days of childhood are seemingly coming to an end. Adolescents naturally have great curiosity, unless it has been dimmed by a dull education or overly strict parenting. Adolescents naturally want to explore, to discover and find their unique identity, place and direction in life. The adolescent still has needs that relate to gaining acceptance as they seek out their direction and purpose in life. When a person gets stuck in adolescence and cannot move to the next phase, they seem like an actor locked into a particular role. Then they are no longer themselves but merely their biography. This is an habitual way of being – the party animal gets drunk, acts outrageously and sleeps around, the tough guy acts hard and picks fights, the sexy young woman acts soft and seductive. Adolescence is a time for getting stuck in a role. Adolescence is a naturally curious phase and so people who get stuck in the adolescent stage can easily feel bored. The entertainment industry panders to people stuck in adolescence, with a whole range of books, websites, TV programmes and videos aimed at alleviating their boredom. Adolescents love new technology and can spend ages obsessively texting friends, and watching gory/slushy movies. Adolescents are increasingly exposed to information overload, leaving little time for personal thought, reflection, or even just 'zoning out'.

Adolescence is a vulnerable time when aggression, competition and busyness can get locked in as ongoing ways of being. The adolescent is often a great rebel, because it is a way of seeking out an identity that is separate from others. The rebel likes to stick his/her fingers up to authority and in moderation this can be a healthy thing. When taken to extremes the adolescent can become quite rigid and inflexible by seeing the world in terms of black and white and of right and wrong.

There are plenty of adults stuck in this phase of development. They are the go-getters, the achievers, the eternal rebels who hate authority. When a company is led by an independent person, the people in that company may well suffer. When a nation is led by an independently-minded person, that nation (and others) is likely to suffer; wars are fought and empires built by independently-minded people.

People who are stuck in the stage of independence fear being dependent. They get stuck in the role of who they think they are. They do not know their true selves anymore, which may feel like a distant memory. They have put on the mask and then forgotten that they are wearing it. Independently-minded people make very good martyrs! They take on heavy workloads and then self-righteously struggle, suffer and inwardly complain about their lot. They take on demands and then feel burdened. They want to be appreciated but often feel that this is not the case. They can do the 'I've worked my fingers to the bone' routine to a tee. Martyrs make the blame game a subtle art form. They take on responsibility for things that are none of their business. They confuse love with duty and sacrifice. Martyrs do not believe in honouring their own needs, nor those of others. They operate from the protestant work ethic which believes in hard work as the way to redemption and happiness. Cut-throat capitalism thrives on martyrs because they make excellent drones. Martyrs work hard, suffer and struggle in life and resent every minute of it.

One of the key aspects of integrating the independent mindset successfully is the creation of healthy boundaries. Symptoms of unhealthy boundaries include: conformity (where a person feels that they must follow other people's rules and think, speak and act according to the norm); withdrawal (building emotional walls to protect their space, shutting out the world); passive aggressive behaviour (keeping people at a distance through silent anger); ignoring reality (which involves blanking out, being overly passive, feeling invisible, suppressing feelings, and hoping that stressful situations will just go away); rebellion (violently defending their space against real or imaginary wrongs); and feeling strangled (where there has been smothering, lack of privacy and intrusion during the formative years).

The signs of having healthy boundaries include the ability to: maintain emotional and physical space from other people when desired; set limits in relation to others; maintain a sense of personal identity, uniqueness, and autonomy (i.e. feeling free to think, feel, create, resolve problems, or act according to one's own wishes without transgressing the boundaries of others); and being able to take responsibility for attitudes, choices, and actions.

Boundaries allow us to rejoice in our own uniqueness and allow for flexibility in relationships. Healthy boundaries allow for closeness and distance; they protect a person from abuse and permit real intimacy.

Clear boundaries are very useful at work, when dealing with money, or in any form of business agreement or transaction. It is important to have clear communication and agreements. Strong boundaries honour our sense of self-worth and prevent us from underselling our time, energy and talent.

Healthy Boundaries

To what degree are your space, privacy, and rights important to you?

What is your set of personal limits that you expect other people to respect?

What boundaries are important to you?

What are the signs that your boundaries have been ignored or violated?

How good are you at handling rejection, in dealing with intimacy, at taking risks, in being assertive, or in handling confrontation?

What is your default strategy for maintaining your boundaries and in what circumstances does it not work?

Start to notice how other people protect their space, autonomy and sense of self. What can you learn?

Practise the simple art of saying 'yes' and 'no' and meaning it.

Prosperity = Living Values

There was a seeker who was told to go to a crossroads, where he would find what he was seeking. He ran to the crossroads and found three shops. One was selling pieces of metal, another wood and the third thin wire. Disappointed, he wandered off and, in time, forgot about his search. One night, as he was walking in the moonlight, the sound of beautiful sitar music filled the air. It was played with such mastery and inspiration that, profoundly moved, the man moved towards the player. He looked at the fingers dancing over the strings and became aware of the sitar itself. Suddenly, he exploded in a cry of joyous recognition; the sitar was made of pieces of metal, wood and wire. He remembered the three shops which he had thought to have no particular relevance. Separately, the items had no meaning but, when put together, there was a synthesis of something much greater than the three separate parts.

The prosperity game is about being an adult in the world; it is about truly growing up. This does not mean that we ditch our dependent and independent parts; that would be repression and denial. The adult honours the child and adolescent parts within and acts as their wise guardian. The dependent child self has a sense of play and creativity. The independent adolescent self has a sense of curiosity and exploration. We do not want to throw the baby out with the bathwater. The adult is conscious of having a whole family of selves inside. We each have many different aspects to our personalities, from the rebel to the pleaser, from the achiever to the control freak. We do not become a conscious adult by denying our selves but by compassionately accepting and embracing them.

The adult mindset flowers in the acceptance of one's own life and achievements. It is a mindset which has successfully integrated needs, feelings, and boundaries. More than this, it is a place of living from a set of meaningful values. In the scarcity game, values are subordinated to making money. The interdependent mindset embraces a broader set of values. There is a true story about a property developer who, in 1989, wanted to build a skyscraper in Frankfurt, Germany. The difficulty was that next to the site lived a woman who had the power to veto the project. She was offered 1 million Deutschmarks, then 10 million. She told the papers that she would not accept even if they offered her 20 million. Her reason was that the skyscraper would block out her sunlight and spoil the place where she grew up.

True adults are a rare breed in this world. They are not greatly understood or appreciated in the scarcity game. The adult has learnt the true value of things and is not willing to give them up, no matter how much the scarcity game offers. The scarcity mindset embraces vague and dubious pseudo-values such as morality, hedonism and elitism. Thus is the scarcity game generated and maintained.

The adult seeks to live by a code of carefully examined values. These are what make our lives valuable; they are the pointers that guide our choices and direct our lives. The most fundamental value we can adopt is to value ourselves – our time, ideas, emotions, choices, mistakes, friendships, romantic relationships, and our work. When we do this, we can then value other people and then other things, such as money. It is surprising how many people want money but do not really value it.

Money can either support or damage our core values. One very wealthy man I met some years back had a deep love for art. He collected paintings and sculptures. When he spoke about them, it was clear that he had a real passion for them. He yearned to be an artist but believed that it was not possible. Instead, he made a lot of money out of the insurance business and sat in his home, admiring his artwork. In time, the stress of making money in a job that he had little passion for made him seriously ill.

It is important to acknowledge and accept the values of others even if we do not agree with them. When we look down on another's values we are not willing to acknowledge that they have the right to live how they please. We are then living from a place that our value set is the only way to live.

In order to acknowledge our true values, we must first question (and, if necessary, replace) the values which we have adopted from others, our parents, guardians, teachers and peers. Only by asking ourselves the question, 'What do I truly value?' can we start to peel away the values that we have unconsciously adopted from others. When Stephen was young, the importance of the value of security was impressed upon him. This informed his working life for many years until he discovered his own values. John was encouraged by his father to be a musician. His father was a frustrated musician in that he loved to play but worked with computers. Jane wanted to follow a career in the arts but her parents persuaded her to study economics. After 15 years of working in the world of finance she discovered that she really wanted to pursue something radically different. If we are not following our values we will not feel a passion for what we are doing. Even if we are financially successful, we will not feel fulfilled. We only feel fulfilled when we start to inhabit our own destiny and 'walk the talk'.

The Values Formula

In the scarcity game, the formula is: if I have the things I want, I can do the things I like and then I can be or feel the way I want.

In the prosperity game, this formula is turned around: if I value what I am, I can do the things that matter to me and then have the things that I enjoy.

Start with values: this is the place of being. From there, begin to act differently. This will lead you to different results.

There are many examples of people who have risen beyond the narrow value of seeking personal gain to make a difference in the world. For instance, Eleanor Roosevelt was the only daughter of an alcoholic father and a beautiful but aloof mother. Although painfully shy and lacking in self confidence for most of her life, she became one of the most loved and revered women of her generation. When Mrs. Roosevelt came to the White House in 1933, she understood social conditions better than any of her predecessors and she transformed the role of First Lady accordingly. She had a deep commitment to social reform and put her energy into a variety of reformist organizations. In the process, she discovered that she had talents – for public speaking, for organizing, for articulating social problems. She gave a voice to people who did not have access to power. She was the first woman to speak in front of a national convention, to write a syndicated column, to earn money as a lecturer, to be a radio commentator and to hold regular press conferences. She walked in the slums and ghettos of the world, not on a tour of inspection, but with real empathy.

Acting from a place of values needs courage as being ourselves sometimes brings condemnation from others. Mae West was born in Brooklyn in 1893; she had a bold and brazen side that challenged many of the female stereotypes of her day. She spent much of her youth and teens in the theatre world, which at that time was dominated by vaudeville shows. She was a performer who exuded an aura of toughness and sexuality. She was considered vulgar by the social elite but popular with those looking for raunchy comedy. As her performances became increasingly popular and notorious, the censors began to take an interest in her acts. In 1927, after a police raid was conducted against her show because she was considered to have offended public morality, the show was ironically given a great boost. The publicity surrounding her arrest and imprisonment for ten days gave her nationwide exposure. She went into the movies and was a great hit. She lived during a time when women who were overtly sexual were held in low esteem. Mae West stated with confidence, 'I'm a girl who lost her reputation and never missed it.' In the late 1930s, Mae West was the most highly paid woman in U.S. movies.

Being values-driven means continually re-evaluating and redefining each aspect of our lives, from relationships to direction to the meaning of achievement and accomplishment. In our twenties, achievement might take the form of academic qualifications and money for leisure, socializing and travel. In our thirties, our priorities may change and we might be more concerned with settling down, getting a home and having a family. In our forties, we might re-evaluate our ideas about success and perhaps opt for a change in direction or a return to study. Whatever stage of development we are at, moving into the prosperity game is a journey which will bring a deeper sense of connection to our authentic self.

Values are as numerous as the stars in the night sky. They are intangible and subtle, with many nuances. Values are both internal states which we can nurture and cultivate and things which we can witness in the actions of others. For instance, it was a sense of justice and compassion that moved the singer Bob Geldof to do something about the plight of people suffering the famine in Ethiopia in 1984. He teamed up with a number of popular musicians under the name of Band Aid, recorded and produced a fundraising single and then went on to raise money through a Live Aid concert. This was hosted on live TV around the world via satellite links and raised millions of pounds for Africa.

The business world understands the importance of values. Andrew Carnegie was born in Scotland in 1835. He went to the United States with his family in 1848 and settled in Pennsylvania. He worked his way through a succession of jobs until, in 1865, he went into business for himself and eventually set up the Carnegie Steel Company, in Pittsburgh. At the age of sixty-five, he sold the company for $480 million and devoted the rest of his life to his philanthropic activities and to writing. Carnegie was perhaps the first to state publicly that the rich have a moral obligation to give away their fortunes. He believed that all personal wealth beyond that required to supply the needs of one's family should be administered for the benefit of the community. Before his death in 1919, Carnegie had given away over $350 million.[2]

Paul Newman created a company to produce salad dressings, pasta sauces, salsas, popcorn, and lemonade. Newman attributes the extraordinary success of his food company to two ideas. The first is that the best ingredients are used without the addition of any artificial preservatives and the second is that all profits, after taxes, are given to educational and charitable organizations. Over $150 million has been donated since 1982.[3]

When media magnate and billionaire philanthropist Ted Turner created the United Nations Foundation in 1997, he pledged $1 billion of his own money to support U.N. programs, including initiatives to protect children in the less developed world from diseases such as measles, malaria and polio.[4]

Thomas Schelling was given the 2005 Nobel Prize, in part for showing that people tend naturally to cooperate more than traditional economic theories have believed. Similarly, one of the original developers of the

World Wide Web, Tim Berners-Lee, turned down offers from a major corporation to develop the Web for profit, and thus helped to launch a new era of openness, freedom and unprecedented wealth creation. Another open-minded entrepreneur, Linus Torvalds, created free *Linux* open-source software that is now run by many large companies, financial institutions and governments. Other companies, such as the U.S. based Whole Foods Market, have a transparency policy around employees' pay so that injustices can be clearly seen and quickly rectified.

In 2000, Farouk Jiwa co-founded Honey Care Africa, a company that trains subsistence farmers in beekeeping. Bees pollinate the countryside which helps agricultural production, they feed themselves and they gather nectar from wild blossoms, which gives an incentive to leave the wild forests intact instead of cutting them down to make charcoal. In a country where half the population lives on 50 cents a day, Jiwa's company is making a difference to thousands of lives.

On the other hand, not living from our core values can have painful consequences. Take the case of Gerald Ratner, the chief executive of Ratner's Jewellery. His infamous speech at the Institute of Directors, where he described his merchandise as 'total crap', caused an estimated billion dollars to be wiped off the company value and eventually sent it into receivership.

Under the presidency of Bill Clinton, the U.S. enjoyed peace and prosperity, together with greatly reduced levels of unemployment, inflation and crime. He proposed the first balanced budget in decades and achieved a budget surplus. Yet, in 1998, as a result of a sexual indiscretion, Bill Clinton was impeached by the House of Representatives and was tried in the Senate. The scandal was highly publicized and caused much suffering for all involved.

Google, the company that could do no wrong, lost 9% of its share value (a massive £13 billion) in one week due to a number of concerns, including its decision to agree with the Chinese government's wish to censor access to Chinese users.[5] As we can see, any lapse in values can prove costly.

What do you Value?

What qualities of being do you value?

Abundance, acceptance, action, adaptability, adventure, aliveness, aspiration, awareness, balance, beauty, boldness, brilliance, challenge, clarity, commitment, compassion, courage, creativity, empathy, equality, expression, flexibility, forgiveness, freedom, fulfilment, generosity, groundedness, growth, happiness, harmony, healing, honour, illumination, imagination, inner power, innovation, insight, integration, integrity, intelligence, intuition, joy, laughter, lightness, logic, love, nobility, openness, passion, peace, persistency, play, precision, purity, purpose, radiance, reflection, self-discipline, self-realization, sensitivity, service, spontaneity, stillness, success, synergy, transformation, trust, truth, warmth or wisdom?

(Please add any quality that is not mentioned).

Pick the three most important values. What makes these so important to you?

When one person awakens a powerful value, the whole world takes a step towards prosperity. A friend of mine who is an executive coach was coaching someone from an investment bank who wanted to change careers but felt that he needed some more capital behind him before he made the move. My friend asked how much he earned in a year and the reply was around £100,000. This person was experiencing a conflict between his need for security and his valuing of freedom and growth. Whenever we experience a conflict of values, it is usually because of a conflict between an adopted value and our authentic value. We may yearn for one thing while something else may have been impressed upon us. This is a conflict between heart and head. If we listen only to our head, we ultimately lose. The heart is the compass that points the way. Heartfelt values are something that ignites us on the inside; they are not simply a good idea. A value needs to be felt in order to be compelling. If a value inspires no real passion, it is not one of our values.

In the book, *The Millionaire Mind* (Bantam, 2002), the author Thomas Stanley researched the psychology of being a millionaire. He questioned over 700 millionaires on their attitudes, beliefs and lifestyles. A common belief held by this group was that the way to sustainable wealth and an enjoyable life is through doing work for which you feel a passion. This is based on the idea that the more you love your work the more likely you are to excel at it, and the more rewards that will be accrued to you. Alexander was earning a high six figure income on Wall Street. He felt no personal satisfaction in his work and dreaded going to work each day. Alexander wanted to be a writer but his family and friends kept trying to convince him how fortunate he was. One day, he picked up a book called *How to Find the Work You Love* by Laurence Boldt (Penguin, 2004), which led him to resign from his job and is now spending each day doing what he loves. The interesting thing is that he went on to make more money writing than he ever did on Wall Street.

Value Zones

Which areas of activity are most important to you: architecture, the arts, business, community, consciousness, education, emotions, empowerment, environment, family, health and well-being, human rights, justice, knowledge, meditation, money, personal growth, philosophy, poetry, psychology, psychotherapy, relationships, science, sexuality, spirituality, sports, story-telling, teaching, team-work, voice, work, or writing?

Write about the things you find important.

What difference would you like to make in the world?

Values are a vital clue in discovering our life's work. You may be a lawyer or a social worker because you believe in fairness and justice. You may be working in publishing or journalism because you love creative ideas. You might be a teacher or youth worker because you want to make a difference to the lives of young people. In the prosperity mindset, work is not about *what* we are doing but about whether or not we are living and engaging in work that is aligned with our core values.

Money is not the most important issue at work. Prosperity is as much about challenge, growth, and purpose as it is about financial reward. Can you imagine doing work that encourages the development of your talent and stimulates within you an 'I can do' attitude? How about work that encourages fun, laughter and play? Can you imagine working in a place where appreciation is a core value?

Deepak was a business trainer who discovered that he had a growing passion for working to protect the environment. Damien left accountancy to follow his passion for internet marketing and coaching. Richard also left accountancy, and became a graphic designer, Alexander Technique teacher and a workshop leader on sacred clowning. Tom was a media executive who travelled the world before giving in to his calling to be an artist. Nick was once a successful computer salesman before becoming a successful author, public speaker and e-product entrepreneur. Ursula went from being an account manager in a publishing firm to being a healer and shamanic practitioner. Alice was a freelance editor who went on to writing romantic novels. Richard went from being an actor to running his own business in corporate training. Johann was a classical music conductor who retrained to be an airline pilot. Beatrice went from being a shop assistant to a successful freelance yoga teacher. Benjamin went from being a concert violinist to working as a healer and then a corporate coach and successful author.

Tim Smit, the founder of The Eden Project, is driven by values. Through his passion and single-mindedness, he turned a disused china clay pit in southern Cornwall into a 'green cathedral'. The Eden Project is helping to keep the living green inheritance of the planet safe for future generations and has attracted over 2 million visitors since it opened its doors in 2001.

Jaime Lerner became mayor of Curitiba in Brazil in 1971 when the city was suffering from a booming population and a huge garbage problem. Garbage trucks were unable to cope and this led to the spreading of disease throughout the city. This mayor decided to do something different. He placed trash barrels around the edges of the shanty towns and everyone who filled them received a free bus token. Schools participated and received free books in exchange for filled barrels. In three years, 100 schools picked up 200 tons of garbage and received 1.9 million books. Seventy percent of the shanty town households became involved in the scheme and the system spurred economic activity in the city. Between 1975 and 1995, the economy of the city grew by around 50%. In 1992, the United Nations honoured the city with the title of 'the world's most ecological city'.[6]

The values-led life is meaningful; it has direction and has more possibilities available to it than a financially abundant yet meaningless life. Values are the keys that unlock our tremendous inner potential. Yet values need to be articulated in some way in order to be made real in the world. We make our values real by speaking about them. We make them real by acting on them. The most extraordinary individuals that have ever lived on our planet were extraordinary not because they had high values but because they were willing to live them and express them at every opportunity.

Values are our pointers towards the prosperity game. They point the way out of lack to abundance: from oppression to freedom; from fear to courage, and from misery to happiness. Embracing values is not an intellectual exercise: values cannot be taught except through example. They cannot be scientifically discovered; they are awakened from the inside out. No-one can tell us our values, although some people can help us find them. We know when we are living by a true value because not only are our actions different, but we feel different about the way we move in the world. People also tend to respond differently to a person who is acting from a place of authentic values. Values are energizing; when we are living them, we no longer feel confused, dull and lifeless. It is challenging to live from a place of values. Life is never dull or static. When we are a living embodiment of our values then life becomes a wonderful adventure into the unknown.

Review Your Values

Review your values regularly (perhaps once every 2–3 months).

Check whether your values remain the same over time or whether they change.

Adjust all courses of action so that they remain in line with your values.

Check whether your actions are in line with your priorities.

References

1. Rosenberg, Marshall. *Non-Violent Communication.* Puddle Dancer Press, 2003
2. http://en.wikipedia.org/wiki/Andrew_Carnegie
3. http://www.motherearthnews.com/Livestock_and_Farming/ 2004_February_March/Using_Money_to_Make_Change
4. http://edition.cnn.com/US/9709/18/turner.gift/
5. http:// news.bbc.co.uk/1/hi/technology/4647398.stm
6. http://www.commondreams.org/views05/1108-33.htm

Chapter 6

Prosperity = Real Thinking

We are what we think. All that we are arises with our thoughts.
With our thoughts we make our world.

THE BUDDHA

There is a story of a wise traveller who rode into a desert village one evening as the sun was setting. Dismounting from his camel, he asked one of the villagers for a drink of water. 'Of course,' said the villager and gave him a cup of water.

The traveller drank the whole cupful. 'Thank you,' he said. 'Can I help you at all before I travel on?'

'Yes,' said the young man. 'We have a dispute in our family; perhaps you can help.' The villager went on to explain that he was the youngest of three brothers. His father had died recently and left seventeen camels. He had decreed in his will that one half of the herd was to go to the eldest brother, one third to the middle brother and one ninth to the youngest. This was the problem: how were they to divide a herd of seventeen?

'Take me to your house,' said the wise traveller.

When he entered the house, he saw the two other brothers and the man's widow sitting around the fire arguing. The youngest brother interrupted them and introduced the traveller.

'Wait,' said the traveller, 'I think I can help you. Take my camel as a gift. Now you have eighteen camels. One half goes to the eldest, that's nine camels. One third goes to the middle son, that's six camels. And one ninth goes to my friend here, the youngest son. That's two camels.'

'That's only seventeen camels altogether,' said the youngest son.

'Yes. By a happy coincidence, the camel left over is the one I gave to you. If you give it back to me, I will continue my journey.'

And he did.

Principle Six   *We generate prosperity to the degree in which we think expansively, creatively and intelligently.*

Prosperity = A Space to Think

The most remarkable tool we have for creating a prosperous reality is our conscious mind. Scientists estimate that the human brain contains some 100 billion neurons. It is a remarkable piece of biological engineering. The human brain has evolved and grown dramatically over the past 3 million years. Relative to body size, humans have the largest brains on the planet. Through this piece of equipment we analyze, plan, perceive, conceive, structure and take things apart: in short, we think. We use our minds to create a hell or a heaven on earth. Every building or city that we see in the world was first conceived in the mind. Every experience we encounter was first dreamed of in the mind. First we think about war, then we wage war. First we think about starting a new project, then we do it. Things do not just happen in the world: they are first created in the mind.

The quality of our thinking is popularly linked to cleverness, yet there are many clever and well-educated people who do stupid things. Nuclear weapons are very intricate and require remarkably detailed conception in the mind before being birthed in the world. Yet the development of nuclear weapons is not a sign of real intelligence. Ask most people and they will tell you that the more nuclear weapons there are on the planet, the less safe we all are.

In order to create a good foundation for innovative thinking, we must take a tip from the computing world and create more space on the hard drive. Just as a computer needs memory space in the hard drive to function well, so does our brain need space, too. If we overload our minds with too much information, it slows down our ability to process it and think creatively. There is no scarcity of information in the world, yet our capacity to hold information consciously is limited. It is important to realize that most of us hold far too much information in our heads than is good for us. In the Western world we are bombarded with information and ideas; this can create mental clutter which, in turn, encourages confused and scattered thinking. It is important to tidy up the contents of our mind from time to time. The more unclosed loops we have in our thinking, the weaker will be our focus. The more 'maybe', 'perhaps', 'could be', or 'it depends' there is in our internal decision making process, the more mental energy it will take to keep all the plates spinning. Most people who have difficulty in making decisions have too many options to choose from and do not know how to make effective choices. To clean up our mental clutter, we need to set priorities; anything that is not important needs to be filed away for future reference. Only the most important things should be occupying our mental space. We need to find ways to contain all the detail so that we can get on with the job of dealing with the bigger picture.

De-Frag Your Mind

To de-frag the mind, start to unload all the data you hold in your head into some appropriate containers. Use a diary, an email inbox, a computer, manual files, and mind-maps – anything that gets all non-essential data out of your head.

Make it a habit not to collect information in your conscious processing space. Be discerning in the information you collect. Prioritize information. File non-important stuff away.

Make a list of all the things about which you have been putting off making a decision. Decide whether each one needs a decision or action within the next week. Write 'yes', 'no' or 'not sure' against each item. Take 'yes' entries and decide which ones can be acted upon now and which need more input of some kind. Take appropriate action and leave everything else for another occasion of your choosing. Repeat the exercise when you are ready.

Prosperity = Thinking a Certain Way

Our state of being and becoming is determined by our thinking. When we think about our problems, our whole being and behaviour is coloured by our problems. This aspect of the scarcity mindset makes life resemble a series of problems to be solved. This habitual way of thinking and being is called problem-oriented thinking. We should not ignore our problems, but it does not help to become fixated on them.

Problem-oriented thinking focuses on what's wrong or what could go wrong. It scans the horizon and misses the beautiful sunrise and notices instead the cracks in the pavement and the piece of litter blowing in the wind. In moderation, this can be a useful because this type of thinking is looking for the potential pitfalls in order to avoid them. When taken to extremes, however, it not only makes us feel bad, it makes other people around us feel bad also. When we habitually focus on what is wrong in a situation, we will miss the not-so-obvious opportunities that are embedded within it.

I once attended a talk by a Zen Buddhist who illustrated this point by showing a video clip of two teams playing basketball. He asked the audience to count the number of times one of the teams passed the ball to each other. After the film, he asked the audience if anyone had seen anything unusual. Of an audience of nearly two hundred people, only a handful said that they had noticed anything odd. He then replayed the clip, asking the audience to watch normally. This time, everyone saw someone dressed in a gorilla suit walk among the players, wave at the camera and then move on. Most people were so focused on the task in hand that they missed the person in the gorilla suit. Problem-oriented thinking is like that. The longer we stay in problem-oriented thinking, the less time we have for possibility or opportunity-oriented thinking. This can be hard to grasp because we are mostly taught that intelligence is the ability to solve problems. Many people have jobs which require them to solve other people's problems. Possibility-oriented thinking means teaching our minds new tricks, to think in a different direction. When we change our thinking, we will not only perceive a different world, we will experience a different world.

One property developer looked at his business as a series of problems to be solved. As soon as one set was dealt with, another would inevitably arise. He attended a personal development training course which helped him to see how this pattern limited him. This one revelation completely turned his business around. In the following two years, he increased his company's turnover by 350%. He attributed his success to reducing the amount of time he spent dealing with problems and increasing the time he spent contemplating possibilities.

Possibility-oriented thinking is not the same as positive thinking. It is not necessary to eradicate every negative thought. In fact, there are no negative thoughts, just ones that will not help you reach where you want to go. Positive thoughts can be defined as the thoughts that help us to go where we want to go, or to achieve what we want to achieve or experience what we want to experience.

There is a true story about a visionary entrepreneur who would not entertain a negative thought. This man was the owner of a property company who had a philosophy of positive thinking and visioning. None of the employees felt able to challenge his visions even when they made little financial sense. His vision propelled the company into a state of constant expansion; his thinking did not allow consolidation and integration, and the company soon lurched into financial difficulties. His answer to this was to expand even more. The last I heard, he was opening another office and taking on more staff. I am not sure whether his business survived his ongoing positive outlook.

I have noticed in business that the most successful teams in terms of working well together creatively and profitably always have a combination of outcome-oriented and problem-oriented thinkers. The ideal combination is where visionary outcome-oriented thinkers lead the way but take heed of the problem-oriented thinkers who can see the challenges that their visions will most likely encounter. The visionaries can then adjust their strategy accordingly. This helps to make the vision more achievable.

In one company I worked in, one colleague would always begin his opening comments on any proposed project or new idea with, 'The one small problem I see with that is...'. Although it was a standing joke in the company, that person was performing a vital role. However, any organization that is dominated by problem-oriented thinkers will tend to be less creative and less able to take measured risks. One organization was dominated by problem-oriented thinkers. Some years previously, the organization had followed a more visionary route but had not taken heed of the problem-oriented thinkers and had been badly burnt financially. They have been afraid of visionaries ever since.

Real thinking is merely a process of laying out a series of stepping stones that head in the direction we wish to go. Yale University carried out a study[1] in which they surveyed a number of their graduates in the 1950s and again twenty years later. Their research showed that 3% were worth more in terms of wealth than the other 97%. The 3% also had better relationships, and were healthier than the larger group. The research discovered that the difference between the groups was not determined by gender, parental wealth, career selected, ethnicity, or any other obvious factor. The difference was that the smaller group had started out with clearly defined goals.

To create a more prosperous personal life, it is important to make room for outcome-oriented thinking. This is where most of our thinking is directed towards what we want. None, or very little, of our thinking should be engaged in what we do not want. However, we must ensure that we are dwelling on the outcomes that we really desire.

A friend of mine had a father who, in the mid-1970s, pursued the dream of becoming a millionaire by the time he was thirty. Although he was being quite successful, it did not quite happen and so he gave up soon after. Having released this dream, he went on to do what he wanted to do with his life; he lived in France for a while and travelled the world.

He was simply chasing the wrong dream. When he let go of the false dream, he could discover what he really wanted to do.

Although pursuing the wrong dream can lead to some dead ends, it is better than having no dream at all. People who are excessively problem oriented tend to think about avoiding difficulties and pain and so avoid pursuing any big dream. This is because they believe it could bring them lots of challenge, heartache and disappointment. Often, problem-oriented thinkers do not believe that reaching their goals is possible.

There are three beliefs that are fertile ground for outcome-oriented thinking: we must believe that our outcomes are possible, that we are capable of achieving them and that we deserve to have them happen. Outcome-oriented thinking is a skill that we can develop with practice. When applied to issues around time, it can be a case of asking oneself: What needs to be done this morning? What are the desired outcomes for the next scheduled meeting? When is the best time to discuss a particular issue to have the greatest chance for moving forward? And it can include the bigger picture such as: Where do I want to be living next year? What level of income do I want to achieve in the next five years? What business would I like to create? The practice of focusing will leave you feeling more constantly energized and excited. The importance of knowing your outcomes cannot be stressed enough. The more clearly the outcome can be seen, heard and felt internally, the better. Outcomes must be stated in the positive, not in the negative. It might be useful to know that you do not want to work as a admin assistant but it would be more useful to know what you do want to do instead.

Have a Big Outcome

One way to work with outcomes is to think about your life in five years' time. Think about how you want to live, what you want to be doing, where you want to be doing it and with whom.

Then think about some goals for the next year that align you with this greater vision. Then think about your goals for the next six months that align you with your vision for the year. Then think about goals for the next month that align you with the next six months. Then think about your goals for the next week that align you with the goals for the month.

Think about your goals today; how do they align with what you want in five years' time?

Great Questions: Great Outcomes

Asking questions is a powerful way to facilitate change, clarify meaning and increase choices. When we do not know the answer to a question, we begin an internal and external search for the answer. Questions are provocative and, if we ask the right ones, they can lead to a questioning of what we think we know and what we think is possible or desirable.

The most useful questions ask 'what?'. 'What?' questions seek information and, more importantly, can elicit desired outcomes. The next most useful questions ask 'how?' 'How?' questions explore process and elicit information and strategies for moving forward. Avoid asking questions which ask 'why?'. 'Why?' questions tend to be used to seek justification for actions and to allocate blame.

Prosperity = Bright Thinking

When we think, it is not in comic-book terms with little balloons filled with words. We think in terms of pictures, sounds, touch, smell and taste. Most people think visually; you will commonly hear them say things like, 'I see what you mean.' People who have a more auditory bias often say, 'I hear what you are saying,' while those who think kinaesthetically speak of 'grasping' concepts and 'getting the hang of' things. These are all sensory terms. We think in ways that connect to sensory experience.

Thought is powerful: we can change our experience by changing what we think. Using the imagination in visualization has become a familiar technique in sports. High-jumpers, for instance, regularly take the time to imagine themselves going through the steps of jumping higher than they have ever jumped before. Actors use it to create a pathway of a performance that they then just simply step into. Mental rehearsal can strengthen or improve behavioural performance, cognitive thinking patterns and internal emotional states. It can be applied to behavioural performance that requires enacting or improving. Just as an actor might silently rehearse lines for a play, it is possible to run through different real-life scenarios before they happen.

The creative power of imagination has an important role in the achievement of success in any field. What we imagine with faith and feeling comes into being. A lack of understanding of the power of the imagination is responsible for much suffering, difficulty and failure. Visualizing an object or situation, and frequently recalling this mental image, has the power to attract the desired object or situation into our lives. Understanding how to use the imagination correctly can open the door to wealth and success without compromising our values or integrity.

The imagination can be used to plan an event, to conjure up a song or painting, to invent a new piece of technology or to envision a new business. In terms of prosperity, it can be used to see a full life instead of an empty one. For some people, prosperity is about visualizing a fridge full of food, eating in beautiful surroundings, having a wallet or bank account full of money, driving a luxury car. It is important that our outcomes are sensorily specific; we need to be able to say what it would look like, sound like and feel like if we were to achieve the desired outcome. The more specific we can be, the better. For instance, if we want to go on holiday to Hawaii, we will more likely feel excited about it if we can see it in our mind's eye. If we could imagine walking on the sand, swimming in the sea, dancing the Hula and visiting fiery Mount Pele, the more real it will feel. The more passionate we feel about our visioning, the better. Passion is what energizes our imagination. If we have a clear picture of what we want but feel little enthusiasm for it then it is not likely to happen.

John worked in the promotion of other people's events but what he really wanted to do was run his own business and promote himself. He imagined running his own company until, eventually, his excitement overcame his fear of taking a risk. He is now running a successful business helping other people overcome their fear of success. Working with the imagination can help us to envision our lives from a higher perspective. It helps us to rise above the monotony of too much detail and to see a broader, more expansive picture. What we envision can one day become reality. The more we can envision a bright future, the more likely we are to create it. Having a bright imagination leads to feeling more optimistic about life. Successful people usually know how to imagine successfully.

For two years I imagined going to Australia. This made me feel so excited that I just had to go. It was fantastic. The sand was finer and more golden than I had imagined and the sea more beautiful and stronger. Actually going to Australia has helped me to improve my ability to imagine a gorgeous golden sandy beach set against a clear blue sea.

Ryan Hreljac has an impossible dream. His dream is that everyone in the world should have access to clean water. He established the Ryan's Well Foundation at the age of nine. He is now 14 years old. He has risen over £1 million which has helped to build 169 wells providing clean water for around 300,000 people in developing countries in Africa and Central America.[2]

Creating a Dream

Sometimes the dream of your life can be found in the past.
What dreams did you have for your life when you were a young child?
What dreams did you nurture as an adolescent?
What dreams did you have as a young adult?
What aspects of these dreams do you wish to drop and what aspects do you want to continue into the present and the future?

What are the most important qualities that you desire to experience in your life? A sense of clarity, freedom, hope, joy, trust or wonder?

In this moment, what would you like to have turn up in your life?
What kind of opportunities? What kind of people?
What kind of work do you dream of doing?
What kind of area do you dream of living in?

What difference do you want to make in the world?
When you are gone from this world, how would you like your life to be remembered?

What If....

What if you won £100 million tomorrow? How would your life be different?
The first thing that people usually consider is taking care of their loved ones and giving to charity.
Imagine that you have already given away all the money that you need to.
Now what would be different in your life?
What specifically would change? How would your life be different?

The Dream Circle

Draw a large circle on a sheet of A4 (US Letter) paper.

Inside the circle, spend 20 minutes or so writing all your personal dreams and desires. Get specific, such as wanting a house by the sea, a red car and so on.

Also write down all the intangible things and qualities you want, such as more laughter, more joy and more love.

You can include symbols, such as a heart for romantic love, a star for success, a gold coin for money.

During the exercise you can also try writing with your non-dominant hand to give voice to a different part of your psyche.

When you have finished writing inside the circle, start to write outside all the things that you want for the world, such as political harmony, world peace, a clean environment and so on.

Put the date at the top of your dream circle. Keep it safe so you can refer to it in the future. You can repeat this exercise at least every 3 months.

Prosperity = Melodic Thinking

We also think by having conversations inside our head. We speak to ourselves all the time. It is a natural way in which many people think. Sometimes these conversations are conscious; at other times we are hardly even aware that we are talking to ourselves. Some of these conversations simply chatter on unconsciously just beneath our everyday awareness.

Some voices speak of irritation, others of desire; some speak of conformity or safety, others speak of change or unrealized dreams. Sometimes the conversations are revealing, but often they are limiting.

We tend to have critical voices because we have been taught to think critically. From the classroom to the courtroom to the boardroom, we learn that real thinking means being able to win arguments and to find the weakness in our opponents. This results in a psyche full of critical voices which seek to slay us before others do. Limiting self-talk is triggered by many different things. One major trigger for self-talk is changing a habit. When we think about doing something different, our inner voices get disturbed, even a little crazy! Limiting self-talk disturbs our ability to think clearly and can adversely impact on our emotions and physical well-being. Limiting self-talk creates that worried look, the glazed eyes and pale face, nausea or anxious feelings in the pit of the stomach. It can also create confusion and fuzziness in the head, and tightness in the chest, arms and legs. Limiting self-talk can cause someone to withdraw, attack, become controlling or feel depressed. Limiting self-talk stops people from following their hearts and dreams.

Rumi was feeling confused around her work and could not gain any real perspective. She had a job that was not fulfilling her any more and she wanted to focus on a singing career. She was having some conversations with herself but could not hear what the voices were saying. She took the time to tune into these conversations. She began to hear one voice speaking to her about safety and earning enough to pay the rent. Another voice wanted her to be more creative in her life and follow her passion for singing. A third voice simply screamed insults at her. By listening to these voices and articulating what they were saying to a friend, Rumi was able to understand her inner process and come to a clearer space where she could weigh up the options and then decide.

Molly decided to do a sponsored run for charity and set herself the target of raising £700. The day before the run, she realized that she had only raised around £500. This was creating an internal conversation that was giving her a hard time. An inner voice was telling her that the shortfall meant that she was bad and had not kept her commitment. After doing the run, she was told by the organizers that she had raised the fifth highest amount for the charity. She did so well that they awarded her the gift of free Ben and Jerry's ice-cream for a year. Not only did her negative self-talk have no bearing on reality but she was able to auction off the ice-cream to raise money for the victims of the Asian tsunami.

The trick to lessening the impact of critical inner voices is firstly to tune into them in order to hear what they are saying. If we cannot hear them, we cannot stop them. They are like submarines that glide beneath our conscious awareness, ready to shoot torpedoes when we least expect it. Once we can hear the voice, we can decide whether we want to listen to its message. Some voices are habitually fearful, while others might express specific concerns which need to be addressed before action can be taken. A voice of doubt could be the voice of long-standing habit or it could offer some intuitive insight into a situation. Listening to critical inner voices takes practice. Whenever we feel depressed or unhappy, there is usually an inner conversation going on.

Some people have difficulty in listening to their inner voices. Another way to explore limiting self-talk is simply to listen to what comes out of our mouth. Whatever we say, we think first. It is important to listen to what we say to other people. People who criticize others are likely to be self-critical. People who speak to others in loving ways are likely to speak to themselves in the same manner. People who complain and blame others are likely to speak to themselves similarly.

Listen to your Self-Talk

When you feel confused, stuck, upset, or depressed, just stop for a few minutes and listen to the conversation going on in your head.

Listen to where you tell yourself you should do something or where words such as **duty** or **obligation** appear. Notice voices that urge you to please others or conform in some way to what other people want. Listen to any voices that sound vulnerable, unsure or afraid.

Listen to any conflicting voices. One voice may urge you towards something while another urges restraint. One voice may contain a lot of emotion while another may want to repress the emotion in order not to make a scene.

It is important not to fight with any inner voice. Awareness and acceptance are much better methods to use.

Listen to how you speak to others. Notice any communication that seems to limit others. Notice how you speak about yourself – for example, when you say to yourself things like 'I can't', 'It's impossible', or 'That won't last'.

Our own limiting conversations can be changed through awareness and with self-discipline. Try changing limiting statements into statements of possibility, such as 'I am able to handle this', 'I will find a way' or 'I can always ask for help.'

Using Expansive Metaphors

Listen to the metaphors that you use in your everyday speech. You may hear yourself saying, 'I've reached a dead end,' or 'I'm between a rock and a hard place.' These metaphors are limiting. Play with expansive metaphors, such as, 'I'm going with the flow,' or 'I'm in my element.'

Listen to the metaphors you use when talking about success, work and money. Do you talk in terms of 'cash flow' or 'frozen assets', 'defeating' the opposition or 'killing' the market?

Find metaphors that give you more possibility in these areas. For example, being on a 'hero's journey', 'finding your way through the labyrinth', 'making it to the other side' or being ready for a 'quantum leap'.

Prosperity = Changing Our Thinking

There is a story of a man who was coming home a little tipsy. As he approached his home he reached into his pocket for his keys but found that they are not there. He started to search the street. A policeman was walking along at that moment and saw him on all fours. The policeman asked, 'What are you doing?'

The man replied, 'Looking for my keys.'

'Did you drop them here?' asked the policeman.

'No,' answered the man. 'I dropped them further along the street.'

The policeman looks baffled and was about to speak when the man hastened to add, 'But the light is much better here!'

Changing our perspective can help us to move beyond our perceived problems. For instance, a business consultant friend of mine was hired some time back to work with a group of people in an industry with a very scientific worldview. The product that they were selling was not doing very well. My friend soon discovered the problem; the people in charge thought that other people (their potential customers) were just as persuaded by scientific facts and evidence as they themselves were. His challenge was not to help them find cleverer marketing ploys but to help them see that scientific arguments aren't particularly persuasive to non-scientists. He used every bit of scientific evidence he could find to show them that the scientific viewpoint wasn't as persuasive as they believed. They were shocked to learn that the world held views different from their own.

Neuro Linguistic Programming makes the distinction between the states of being associated and dissociated. These are different ways in which we experience the world. Being associated means thinking of a situation and seeing, hearing or feeling it as if you were right there. Being dissociated is when you experience a situation as an onlooker and feel more distant from it. Being associated is good for learning new skills, for paying attention, and enjoying the moment. Being dissociated is good for reviewing experiences or memories, for separating yourself from unpleasant experiences and for keeping track of time.

People who are phobic are totally associated with their fears; they cannot get any distance from the object of their terror. People who are problem-oriented thinkers tend to be associated into their problem scenarios. They can sense them as if they are standing right before them, blocking their way or else surrounding them like an invisible prison. For those who are associated with their fears and worst case scenarios, hearing a piece of bad news has them imagining all too clearly what it would be like if the same thing happened to them or their loved ones. The scarcity game, via the media, encourages people to associate with their fears. One young woman whom I know was so traumatized after hearing about the London terrorist bombings that she could no longer use London Transport. One day, she was due to go on a training course while her five-year-old son was due to go on a school trip. This trip involved using the underground. During the training course, she could not concentrate and, throughout the day, kept imagining the worst. Eventually, she broke down in tears. Rationally, she knew that her son was safe, but this did not help her.

However, some people are associated with the feeling of wealth or success; when they speak of it, they can see, hear or feel themselves right there as if the situation were happening right now. People who associate themselves with success find it easier to achieve.

The business world is littered with people who are either too associated or too dissociated from their reality. Jack, a friend of mine, ran a very successful graphic design business for many years. He slowly found that he was losing interest in the business and, in time, it folded. He went from bringing in lots of money to very little and gradually started to accrue debts. After a few years, he owed over £25,000. He was very laid back about his debt because he believed that one day he would pay it back. His wife, however, was completely associated into the scenario of debt. She worried constantly about the future. Jack was happily disassociated from the problem while Nancy was unhappily associated into it.

In another case, Nigel was a successful trainer and author and had a clear picture of himself succeeding in his business. His partner Anthea, although more highly trained and qualified than Nigel, was unable to see herself being successful in any one thing. She had tried many things with great enthusiasm at first but nothing had worked out very well. Nigel's success and Anthea's lack of it were largely down to the ways in which they viewed their reality.

One of the benefits of counselling and other talk-therapies is that it helps people to externalize and get a little distance from the problems they associate into inside their heads. Speaking out about a problem can put some space between a person and their limiting thoughts. It is useful for a person in distress to dissociate from their stressful thinking process. Conversely, one of the benefits of visualization techniques is that they help us in associating into positive things that have not yet happened. For someone who has never experienced much intimacy, joy, success or wealth, visualization is helpful in associating into new feeling states.

Someone I knew had recently arrived into the country from Slovenia with his girlfriend. He spoke very little English and also lacked confidence that he would be able to find work. His girlfriend asked for help. During a session, she translated between us and it soon emerged that he was associated into people's criticism of him and dissociated from the feeling of success. In the past, he had felt that his colleagues were jealous of him and so he had held himself back from moving forward. I soon found an image that worked for him. He was a passionate football fan, so I used the metaphor of football to help him to associate into teamwork and success. I had him imagine that he was playing for his favourite team in a packed stadium. I had him imagine in slow motion that he was being crossed the ball into the goal mouth. I then asked him to imagine the play reverting to normal speed and had him kick the ball with full force into the goal. At that moment, he also visualized the whole stadium erupting with joy. He cried with joy, as did I and his girlfriend. The release of energy within him was palpable. He soon got a job with which he was very happy and where his scant English was no barrier.

Learning to associate into the things we want is a very powerful practice which can produce wonders. Visualizing a gorgeous colour, an amazing aroma, a sexy smile, or remembering a happy memory cannot fail to lift the spirits. Being associated into joy rather than misery can be life-transforming. There can be great joy to be found in watching the sunrise, in seeing flowers grow, in having tea with a friend, in doing something that is a bit of a stretch, in being loved and supported by other people, and in making a difference to people's lives. Make it a practice to focus on joy for several minutes every day. Make it a practice to bring joy into the lives of those you know and love. Make it a practice to bring joy into the lives of people you do not yet know.

How about associating into laughter? A friend of mine who runs training courses around work and inspiration has a great exercise around money. He asks seminar participants to get out a note or a credit card and then has them venting for several minutes all the upset and blame they hold against money. Most people find the exercise ridiculous and start laughing. Humour is a great antidote for blame and thinking about problems. Real humour is about laughing with people, not at them. Real laughter makes people more attractive. What things make you laugh? What things do you do that make other people laugh?

Associating into a Quality

Each day, choose one quality into which you want to be associated. Then, throughout the day, look for that quality around you, in the places you go and in the people you meet. Start with a quality which you desire to create more of in yourself.

Imagine how it would look and feel if you lived from that quality. If the quality is joy, for instance, how would it feel to live joyfully? What would you be doing as a joyful person throughout the day? How would you relate to others from a place of joy?

Repeat as often as you like.

The more you do it, the better the results.

References

1. http://www.iamnext.com/living/goals.html
2. http://positivenewsus.org/content/home/news/samplestor/pickadream/default_html

Chapter 7

Prosperity = A Deep Mythology

If you want one year of prosperity, grow seeds.
If you want ten years of prosperity, grow trees.
If you want one hundred years of prosperity, grow
people.

CHINESE PROVERB

Orpheus, son of Apollo and the muse Calliope, was a great poet and skilled musician who could charm birds and animals with his lyre. Orpheus married the Naiad nymph, Eurydice, who met a tragic death on the very first day of her marriage. She trod on a snake and died from the poisonous bite.

The moment she died, all the joy went out of Orpheus's life. He no longer sang of happiness, but of his sorrow. Orpheus, heart-broken, begged Zeus, the Father of the Gods, to restore her. Zeus gave him permission to seek her in Hades, and Orpheus journeyed into the Underworld, playing his music as he went. He passed by the ferryman, Charon, and the three-headed guardian dog, Kerberos, who were both charmed by his music. He passed through the realm of the dead and they wept as they heard him play. Eventually, he presented himself before the thrones of Hades and his wife Persephone. When they heard him play, they were so overcome that they gave him permission to take Eurydice back with him to the land of the living. The only condition imposed by Hades was that, on the return journey, he was not to look back, under any circumstances, until they reached the world above. They left that shadowy kingdom. Comforted and enchanted by the playing of his lyre, Eurydice followed Orpheus through the long, dark passage towards the light of day... .

Principle Seven   *We are all resourceful beings; there is no limit to our inner potential. As we awaken our unconscious resources we can use them to generate prosperity in the world.*

Prosperity = A Deep Power

Prosperity exists deep inside of us all. In the story, Orpheus journeys into realms to which most people are afraid to go. We are going to journey together to the kingdom of the deep unconscious. Yet as Virgil says, 'any fool can go down there'; returning is the difficult part. The story of Orpheus and Eurydice is a metaphor for crossing the threshold between the conscious world of light and the deeper, shadowy world of the unconscious. We know that we have a conscious mind; it is the centre from which we choose, plan and think. But our unconscious mind is deeper and more mysterious. Scientists calculate that our conscious mind can pay attention to around 126 bits of information per second. This may sound like a lot but just listening to another person takes around 40 bits of our 'attention'. Our mind is flooded with information all of the time and we could not possibly process all of it and that is why we have an unconscious mind. The unconscious mind handles everything that the conscious mind does not need to. It keeps the heart beating, the temperature in the body at a constant level, and a thousand and one other activities going. The unconscious retains memories as well as learnt and habitual ways of doing things. When we learn to drive, our unconscious mind is the part of us that is really learning so that eventually we can both drive and do something else at the same time, like chat to a passenger. When we learn to play a musical instrument, it is the unconscious mind that has learnt to do the activity. The unconscious allows us to play without thinking about it. In fact, thinking about any learned activity is likely to get in the way. If we learn to play tennis, it is our unconscious that is doing most of the playing. A tennis ball in flight goes too quickly for our conscious mind to follow; it is our unconscious that tracks the ball and knows how to produce the perfect return.

In order to create a different reality for ourselves and others, it is important to understand the incredible power of the unconscious mind. Freud saw the unconscious as being hidden, like the man behind the curtain in the Wizard of Oz. Freud believed that the goal of therapy was to make the unconscious conscious. The unconscious contains all our memories; it contains our most cherished thoughts, dreams and aspirations and also those things that we despise and fear the most. The unconscious is the realm of the emotions; it is hard to make ourselves angry or sad consciously.

Prosperity = Positive Suggestion

Scarcity and prosperity are both states of ongoing autosuggestion. We unconsciously believe that our lives will turn out in a certain way and then they do. The unconscious has the miraculous power to shape our destiny. We can use this to our advantage. Psychologists have performed many experiments on people in hypnotic trance which have shown the unconscious mind to be suggestible. People in hypnosis stage shows have been made to bark like a dog, slap someone's face, and act out all kinds of bizarre behaviour that they would not normally do in everyday life. The unconscious, if allowed by the conscious mind, will accept any ideas, however uplifting or destructive, and act in accordance with them. Joseph Murphy in his best selling book, *The Power of Your Subconscious Mind* (Pocket Books, 2006) describes the unconscious mind through the metaphor of the garden. He says that the conscious mind is the gardener that plants seeds in the unconscious all day long. We can either plant flowers or poisonous weeds, the procedure is the same. In our garden it is not only our own thoughts that plant seeds but also other people's. In the scarcity game, our unconscious mind is vulnerable to all kinds of marketing ploys designed to hook our unconscious and emotional responses. Many companies manage to sell junk food and drink and other products successfully because they have learnt to manipulate the unconscious mind through media such as TV. The advertising industry has long been aware of the suggestibility of the unconscious. Advertising campaigns are deliberately designed to manipulate our unconscious drives towards pleasurable buying and the avoidance of not having. Linking highly evocative imagery with products over and over again can deeply impress the unconscious. This is why the scarcity game invests millions in advertising. They know it pays dividends.

The power of suggestion can create health or illness. Take the case of a distant relative of the author Joseph Murphy, who visited a celebrated crystal gazer in India. He was told by the seer that he had a bad heart and would die at the next new moon. He was aghast and called all of his relatives and even contacted his lawyer to make sure his will was in order. Joseph tried to talk his relative out of his conviction, but he replied that the seer was known to have amazing occult powers. As the new moon approached, the man became more and more agitated. Just a month before he had been robust and happy but, on the predicted date, he duly suffered a heart attack and died. According to Joseph Murphy, he died unaware that he had caused his own death.

We can learn to clear the unconscious of the weeds of such limiting suggestions. We can start to create a very happy garden for ourselves. Under hypnosis, suggestion has been used for some amazing purposes. Take the case of Dr. Esdaille, a Scottish surgeon who practised in Bengal in the 1840s. He used hypnotic suggestion (anaesthetics had not yet been invented) to conduct 400 major surgical operations between 1843 and 1846 including amputations, removal of cancerous growths and eye operations. His patients felt no pain and no one died during surgery. Just as amazing, the mortality rate after surgery was very low. This was in the days before antibiotics.[1] Suggestion can lead people to walk barefoot across a carpet of red hot coals for some 20 feet or so. I know because I have spoken with people who have done it. None of them felt anything or had any marks on their feet.

How is any of this possible? The answer lies in the power of belief. Beliefs are powerful shapers of our social world, in that they help to shape our thinking, feeling and conduct. Beliefs act as inhibitors or permissions and they tend to be self-fulfilling prophecies. Beliefs influence what we think is possible and also how capable and deserving we will allow ourselves to feel in relation to the things we want in life. If someone believes that they are a failure, or stupid, or a waste of space, the consequences of such beliefs are fairly easy to predict. Beliefs dictate the direction and quality of our thoughts and feelings; in turn, these influence our choices and actions. Beliefs are the foundation upon which we build our lives. The importance of belief cannot be emphasized too much. If we manage to root out just one limiting belief and replace it with a more positive one, our whole reality will shift. Changing limiting beliefs – such as 'nothing works', 'I will never amount to anything', 'I cannot cope', 'I am not very bright', 'I do not have what it takes' – is essential, otherwise we will just see results in our lives that match our limited expectations. The unconscious accepts suggestions about being stupid or brilliant, uncaring or compassionate, rigid or spontaneous and then acts accordingly. Inner resources will be shut down or opened up in line with such accepted suggestions. Persistently thinking in terms of being clumsy or poor, or a failure or a loser will impact on the unconscious.

Where money is concerned, we may believe any number of things: 'It doesn't grow on trees', 'It is hard to come by', 'It only goes to the most deserving' or 'we have to work very hard to get money'. We can believe that money is the root of all evil, or the root of all good; we might believe that it corrupts or that it can solve our every problem. We may believe that there is not enough to go around or that the only way to get money is to cheat the system. We can hold all kinds of beliefs around money: we may think that money comes because of class, gender, race, merit, or self-worth. We might believe that some people are just naturally lucky or successful.

Our unconscious creates our experience. Sometimes, we hold contradictory beliefs that create feelings of stuckness and limitation. One person believed that she was both lucky and unlucky with money. How this reflected in her life was that when she earned some extra money she would also receive some kind of bill which took the extra money away. Sometimes the pattern worked out in uncanny ways. Once, I remember her telling me how happy she was to have earned an extra £500 from doing some design work. A few days later, she received a bill from her local garage of £500 for repair work to her car.

Kate believed that she was not very talented and could not rise above a certain station in her working life. She looked at the origins of the belief and found that, when she was young, she was encouraged to do well academically and did so. Then, when she was doing her A-levels, the emotional support from her parents to achieve vanished suddenly. Inexplicably, they encouraged her to get a job like her brother instead. Her father said that he was no longer prepared to support her financially and that it was time to stand on her own feet. This sudden change turned her world upside down and she felt uncertain about the future. Her dream of going to university vanished and instead she felt launched into the job market. She hated her first job, and the second, and in fact almost every job she has done ever since. What she really wanted to do was continue her learning. Because of this early frustration, she formed a belief that work was uninteresting and repetitive. She worked on changing the belief and started to open to the possibility that work could be a place of creative challenge and learning. She left her old 'boring job' and, in time, found work that enabled her to grow as a person. She discovered new talents in leadership and envisioning and became a director of a new innovative project in the educational field.

Our core beliefs originate in our families during our formative years. When we are young, the unconscious mind is always listening and learning. It listens to the conversations around the dinner table and how the topic of money and other related issues are discussed. The unconscious also reads the unspoken messages, the body language, the look, the tone of voice and the long silences in response to any important issue.

Some beliefs need considerable work to release; they have deep roots since they have been nurtured and reinforced for years. Other beliefs can be released very easily and quickly. As we change our inner assumptions and ways of thinking, the world will relate and respond to us in different ways. Simon had always believed in and experienced a lack of love in his life. This belief had formed in childhood because his father was busy and distant and his mother was often depressed and unable to hug or kiss him. The lack of emotional and physical contact led to a deep-seated belief that love was scarce. The first step in releasing this belief was acknowledging where it came from. Simon confronted the belief in a number of workshops and through written and verbal counter-affirmations. Gradually, the old belief in a 'lack of love' was uprooted and a new belief in the abundance of love was planted. As the new belief took root and was reinforced and nurtured, Simon's relationships changed and the glass ceiling on romantic love lifted as new friends came into his life.

The unconscious is powerful. It can switch off a talent if it believes that this is necessary. For instance, a friend of mine played tennis quite a bit as a teenager. He used to play two or three times a week with a friend and he always won. After some months, he began to feel sorry for his friend and decided to let him win sometimes. He allowed his friend to win two or three matches on the trot and then decided to go for a draw. What he did not realize at the time was that his unconscious had heard the instruction to lose tennis matches and, from that time onwards, his game was not so fluid. He mis-hit shots and his serve was a bit off. He was surprised to find that he lost that match to his friend, and the next and the next. His unconscious had reduced his performance as requested. Since the idea was not deep-rooted, it shifted after a while. Another friend, John, remembers playing chess with his father when he was 14 years old. He remembers the look of shock on his father's face when John won for the first time. That look impressed upon him the idea that winning was not a good thing. In future games he allowed his father to win. Later in life, John found that he was not able to win at very much at all. He began to class himself as a 'loser'. When he tracked this back to the original experience he saw that he had decided early on in life that winning meant hurting other people. As he became more conscious of the belief he was able to change his thinking. He saw that winning did not have to be a bad thing. He saw that winning did not mean that other people get hurt. He is now a successful author.

The unconscious mind is impressed by authority; if an authority figure says something negative about us, the unconscious can take it as a literal truth rather than just an opinion. A parent who consistently tells a child that they are stupid can implant that belief in the child's unconscious. A doctor who tells a patient that they have just six months to live may actually form a belief in the patient's mind that they are going to die.

Fortunately, some people are immune to such messages. After the Great War, my grandfather was told that he had six months to live. He refused to accept this medical opinion as fact and so lived for another fifty years.

The reason that some people are immune to such suggestions is that the natural tendency of the subconscious is towards life. When left alone, the unconscious is very capable; it can run the body, learn a new skill, and remember all manner of things quite well. When the conscious mind gets in the way, whether through worrying or through focusing on problems or through contemplating a limiting idea, it blocks the natural ability of the unconscious to get on with its job. When the conscious mind thinks thoughts like 'I'm confused', 'I see no way out', or 'it's hopeless', the unconscious gets the message and stops trying to be of help.

Undoing Limiting Beliefs

An important principle to remember is that awareness is curative. Simply bringing a limiting belief to consciousness can help to liberate stuck mental and emotional energy.

1. Pick an area where you feel blocked or limited. Find a statement that describes how you feel in this area, such as 'I am a dead loss', 'I cannot stand up for myself', 'I'm a failure', 'I'm unlucky', 'nothing changes', 'I do not deserve to be happy', 'I'll never make it', 'I cannot have what I want', 'I am always broke', 'My life has no meaning', 'money is evil', 'money corrupts', 'I am always in debt', or 'money does not grow on trees'.

2. Now reverse the statement: for instance, 'I am poor' can become 'I am wealthy' or 'I feel wealthy' or 'I am opening to wealth'. The statement should give you a feeling of liberation and possibility and always begin with 'I am...' or 'I feel...'

3. Spend a few minutes each morning just before you get up contemplating the new thought. Repeat at least once during the day and before going to sleep.

4. Take one small action during the day that is in alignment with this new statement. If the statement is 'I am wealthy', how about having a walk around an expensive shop? If it is 'I am a loving person', how about buying a flower for a stranger? Most importantly, be inventive and have fun!

Prosperity = A Personal Mythology

There was a cargo ship that limped into port after developing engine trouble. The crew were unable to find the source of the problem and so they called for a specialist from shore. In time, a little old man hopped on board and began tapping the engine with a small hammer. He tapped and listened. After several minutes he seemed to find what he was looking for and gave a heavier tap to a valve. The engine sprung into life. The man scribbled out his bill and handed it to the captain. '$300!' exclaimed the captain, 'You were here for less than ten minutes and all you did was tap the engine with your hammer.'

The old man replied, '$5 was for the tapping, $295 was for knowing where to tap.'

The unconscious is the engine that drives the ship of our life. When we develop engine problems, one place to tap is our personal story or personal myth. The unconscious communicates to us in dreams symbols, metaphor and through stories. The unconscious adopts one or more stories to make sense of life. To the unconscious, a bad story is preferable to no story at all. Our personal stories shape our everyday interactions and our destiny. They can work for or against us. Our stories are bound together by our deepest beliefs about ourselves and life. They organize our thoughts, feelings, perceptions and actions into a coherent pattern.

Our personal myth comes from our family, which in turn is informed by past family members and the culture in which the family is embedded. Our personal myth is influenced by our schooling and other such experiences but the core of the myth remains a family one. Families are living stories. Unresolved trauma and heartbreak can pass down through the generations to influence the lives of later family members. These living stories affect different family members in different ways. Sometimes, the women are affected in one way and the men in another. They can affect the oldest child in one way and the youngest in another. No matter how much we try and run away from our families, we will take our personal myth with us. I have known people leave their family when they were young and even go to another country but still were unable to escape from the personal myths handed down to them by their families. One young woman left Italy at the age of nineteen and settled in London. She thought that she had left her personal myth behind but, during her twenties, she started to suffer from sleeplessness. When she did sleep she would dream of her family. She had to return to Italy to face her past and unravel her personal myth. Another young woman from Eastern Europe had dominating parents. She felt that the only way to escape from them was to leave the country and settle in another. Again, she had restless sleep and often dreamt that she was back in her homeland and could not leave.

One young woman experienced her father leaving when she was quite young. This meant that self-blame was included in her personal story because she felt directly responsible for his leaving. One young man had an emotionally unavailable mother and a physically unavailable father. Into his personal story was added an immediate sense of a lack of deserving and of rejection. Another man had very critical parents and he learnt to protect himself by withdrawing and not expressing his opinions. Into his personal myth went a sense of being unable to speak his truth.

We are story-telling creatures. Some people's stories are tragic like *Hamlet*, others feature abandonment like the fairy story of *Hansel and Gretel*. Some weave around the themes of love and loss like the story of *Romeo and Juliet*. Some stories may be about imprisonment and waiting, like one of the maidens of old, locked in a tower waiting to be rescued by a gallant knight. Some stories are about revenge, others about guilt. Some are about death and dying. Some feel like emotional roller coasters, others dull and lifeless. Some are about power, others about feeling powerless. Some are about conflict, others about fighting for a cause. Some people's stories are like grand opera, others are more like a TV soap.

Clues to our personal myths can be found in the stories that attract us. We may have a favourite story, or fairy tale, or myth that just speaks to us. I was once staying with a family whose eldest daughter loved the TV soap *EastEnders*. I watched it with her and was completely bored whilst she was totally rivetted. I later chatted with her and discovered how much of her own life was being reflected in the constant drama of the TV series. By watching it, she was being shown a replay of many of the features of her own personal story. This can be tremendously healing for a person who is seeking to understand the hidden themes of their life. Belinda was fascinated by horror films, which helped her to understand the hidden themes of violence and fear in her life.

Peter loved the film *Jason and the Argonauts* and watched it many times when he was a young boy. The film helped him to see the hidden theme of the heroic journey which was to be so important to him later in life. Stephen loved *The Matrix* and watched it over and over. In his family, there were secrets and he grew up with the feeling of not really knowing the truth. The film had a similar theme that reality was not as it seemed. The journey of the central character, Neo, was to understand this hidden reality and to escape from its pre-programmed bounds. The stories that we love to hear in books, films and plays reflect the themes of our personal stories. The characters in these stories can also reflect conscious or unconscious aspects of ourselves.

Elizabeth loved the film *Gone With the Wind* and readily identified with the theme of love being a struggle. She also loved the character, Scarlet O'Hara. In her own life, she had the ongoing experience of falling in love with either the 'wrong' kind of man or one that was totally unavailable.

Our personal story also encompasses the archetypal realm, meaning that it goes beyond our family stories into more universal ones. Archetypal stories involve the king, the queen, the lover, the mother or father, the warrior, the heretic, the ascetic, the hanged man, death, the priestess, the magician and many more. Whatever our personal story, it informs how we see and hear the world, what we think is achievable and what we think is impossible. To work with personal mythology, the first thing we need to do is to find the core themes. Sam had an outlaw story running. She was a rebel in life who could not trust authority. She was unable to settle anywhere for too long and had lots of conflict with people around her. James had a heretic story running and felt persecuted in life. In one job, he discovered that most of the staff were fundamentalist Christians from various groups. His immediate boss was a Born Again Christian who was deeply suspicious of James because he kept his spiritual beliefs to himself. One night James had a dream; in the dream he was a woman who was being taken by a horse-drawn cart to a place of execution. His dream character was being led to a place of burning. He woke up with feelings of extreme terror and rage at the event. This dream was a turning point in his work. He was able to understand his feelings of persecution and how they had woven throughout his life.

Frank had a death temptation story running where he felt a noose was metaphorically around his neck for most of his life. He was living a life waiting for the end. With such a story, he did not seek to start very much in his life; he simply tried to cope and get through the next day.

Some people run saviour stories and spend their lives taking care of others. Their unconscious minds are on the lookout for people who need rescuing. People can get stuck in victim stories because they did not get the love and care they needed as children. They remain stuck, refusing to go forward until they receive the love they need.

The problem in the scarcity game is that many of the old myths by which people used to live their lives have been dismantled or re-shaped. Religion once provided myths to explain the meaning and purpose of life. Mostly these have been replaced by the myths of materialism. Scarcity has warped the ancient myths and turned them into cartoons or computer games. The hero's journey has been reduced by Hollywood to a story where the good guys need to shoot and destroy the bad guys. Myths of spiritual quests have less meaning in a culture of accumulation, control and mindless combat. Myths about Eden, Paradise, and Valhalla have less meaning in a culture dominated by high technology and computer games. In the absence of real myths, the scarcity game creates pseudo-myths. Yet even a pseudo-myth may be better than no myth.

Your Personal Story

Clues to your personal story can be found in the things that you say on a daily basis.
They can be found in the things that you do not say but would like to.

What subjects do you keep talking about?
What themes do you keep returning to?
What things do you want to talk about but dare not?
Write about these themes in your journal.
If there is something you dare not say to others, write about it.

What book, film or play fascinates you?
What is the theme of this story, and who are the main characters?
How does this story relate to your life?

What story would you like to live?
Is it a heroic story, a spiritual story, a love story, a magical story, a community story, or a success story?

Write out the basic theme of the story and the character you would like to play.

It is important to work with personal stories in a way that makes sense to your unconscious. The re-worked story must bear some resemblance to the original story. For instance, a person who has a story of being alone and rejected could work with the ugly duckling story where the baby swan was lonely amongst the other ducks but was no longer lonely when found by his fellow swans. A rebel story could be re-worked along the lines of becoming a heroic Robin Hood. A story of someone who has no purpose could be worked along the lines of the knight Gawain who went out in search of the Holy Grail and found it in the castle of the Fisher King. A woman who has a story that 'it's a man's world' could work with a myth of a powerful Goddess like the Greek Athena or the Egyptian Isis. The myths and stories of all time are there for us to use. Our small, personal story can be woven into a larger more inspiring story. Once we have a large and compelling story to inhabit, life becomes very different. Working with personal stories is not only powerful but a way of being creative and of having lots of fun.

Janet had a story of feeling plain and unattractive. She saw an NLP Practitioner and realized that she had an ugly duckling story running and was stuck in the first part of the story. She moved the story on and became the swan who found other swans to appreciate her. The next day, a friend she had known for a year noticed the difference immediately – so much so that he asked her out for a date on the spot!

Philip had a powerful dream one night in which he was a beautiful woman with long blonde hair and a red evening dress. As the beautiful woman, he caught a bus that was filled with many of his male work colleagues. In the dream he felt very embarrassed and threatened. The dream was revealing his feminine side that had long sought expression in the world. He worked with the image of the woman in the red dress until he felt very comfortable with her. This image had many gifts for Philip. He found that he really enjoyed his feminine side and that she brought him a sense of grace and beauty that he had not felt before. She had a magnetic quality and charm that began to appear in Philip's life. People began to notice that something was different but just could not put their finger on it. However, his wife who knew about the dream commented that she enjoyed his new found 'softness'.

Hannah loved *The Lord of the Rings* so much that she had read it a dozen times by the time she was in her mid-twenties. The story was powerful for her because it touched on the core theme of good and evil, and the adventure of confronting fear. Hannah identified with the reluctant hero Frodo, as well as the loyal Sam. Other characters in the book, such as the noble Aragorn, and the magical and wise Gandalf, represented other aspects of her character that she had yet to awaken. These aspects did awaken in her late thirties when she became interested in shamanism and magic.

Re-Imagining your Story

Imagine stepping on a road that represents your past, present and future. Look along the road in the direction that represents your past. Walk down it and explore using all of the senses. How does it look, sound and feel?

Perhaps a story will unfold along the road; notice the scenery and any characters you meet. Explore your personal story, in all its stuckness or glory.

What aspects of the story that unfolds would you like to change? What aspects would you like to enhance?

Now imagine that you can change anything you like. You can take some things away and enhance others. Imagine the things that you do not want disappearing and the things that you do getting brighter and stronger. Repair the road where necessary: make it wider, smoother, cleaner. Put new things along the road, such as a beautiful house, mansion or castle, include other things such as green fields, or wild woods or whatever else you would like to see.

Now turn to the future and do the same. This time, place your cherished dreams along the road. The ones you want to happen immediately will be closer to you along the road and the more distant dreams will be on the horizon. Brighten the whole road with flowers or with gold sunlight or silver starlight. Be imaginative. Repeat this exercise as often as you can.

Creative visualization is one way in which to discover and interact with the personal myth. It is said that a picture paints a thousand words; both religion and the corporate world have recognized the power of symbols to influence the unconscious. Religion uses imagery such as the cross, the six-pointed star, the chalice, the altar, the candle and so on. All of these symbols are very potent to the unconscious and carry very deep meaning. A personal myth is constructed along a chain of images or symbols. Change just one of the links and the whole chain is different.

For a person with a mythology of restriction, a symbol that conveys a sense of freedom will be powerful. For a person with a mythology of abuse, a symbol of protection will be helpful. For a person with a mythology of feeling powerless, a symbol of inner power will begin to change the core message of their private myth.

Esther was nervous about her driving test. I asked her to close her eyes and ask her unconscious for an image of how she felt about the test. The image was of walking through a difficult and wild landscape. I asked her how she would like to feel – 'like a graceful panther' – and so she changed the image. I asked her then to make the landscape a more pleasant one. She felt a lot better. When she worked on the image some more, it changed into that of the ever so cool Pink Panther. She used this image to help her to pass her test first time.

Julie had grown up with a lot of criticism. Her personal myth was of not being good enough and never really achieving very much. She wanted to do something to help her confidence and some friends suggested she try dancing. She went along but was not able to relax and really get the steps. She was helped to dance and really enjoy it by working with a symbol. In meditation she saw herself as a pathetic dancer with no passion. She changed the image to that of a flamenco dancer full of passion. This image helped her to become a competent dancer.

Symbols Work

Pick an outcome you would like and spend a few minutes contemplating it. You need to set the intention of discovering the most powerful image you can find to represent this outcome.

What images come to mind? Keep allowing these images to come and go. The more compelling the symbol, the better – some obvious examples being a red heart for more romantic love, a silver star for greater success, a soaring eagle for liberation and freedom, a candle for clarity, or a handful of gold coins for increased prosperity.

Stay with the image and allow it to change if it wishes. Keep holding the intention of finding the most appropriate symbol for you. Allow yourself to be surprised by what comes.

When you have found the image, draw it in your journal and say what it represents to you. If you can, draw this image and colour it in and place it on a prominent place on a wall where you can see it each day.

Then, for a few minutes each morning, sit in silence and internally bring to mind the image and set it within an appropriate landscape. Perhaps your candle is set on an altar, perhaps your red heart is set in a garden, perhaps your soaring eagle is above a great mountain. Play with the symbol, have fun, and notice any feelings that arise.

References

1. Murphy, Joseph. *The Power of the Subconscious Mind.* Pocket Books, 2006

Chapter 8

Prosperity = Irresistible Flow

Prayer is a custom, and fasting an affordable act.
You know people through their dealings with wealth.

ARABIC SAYING

There is a true story about a farmer called Al Hafed who lived some years ago in the Persian Gulf. He had a farm on the banks of the River Indus that had bountiful orchards and large fertile gardens, and since the farm was doing well he had enough money to live comfortably. He had a beautiful wife and children and felt very happy and contented with his lot. Then, one day, a visitor came and spoke to him of many things. He told him how the world was first made and he told him about the fabulous wealth that could be found in the earth. He spoke of precious stones and of the great value of diamonds. He told him that with just a few of these stones he could buy many farms and be even more wealthy and contented. Al Hafed listened and suddenly a great unhappiness arose in him. The more he thought about the wealth he did not have, the unhappier he grew. He sold his farm, said farewell to his family and went off in search of precious diamonds. He travelled throughout the Middle East and into Europe but he found no diamonds. After a few years he had squandered all his money and wandered around in rags. One day, a large wave came in and swept him out to sea. The man who had bought Al Hafed's farm fared much better. One day, as he watered his animals in a stream running through his property, he noticed something glinting in the sunlight. It was a beautiful diamond and the farmer had not only discovered a valuable gem but one of the richest diamond fields in history.

Principle Eight   *Prosperity is first an inner possibility before it becomes an outer probability. When we awaken our inner prosperity state we enter into the flow of life.*

Prosperity = Beyond Struggle

When we end scarcity in ourselves, we will see, hear and touch a different world. Scarcity ends not by fighting or demonstrating against it, but by transforming it on the inside first. Prosperity is the natural state of people and the natural world. People and nature are innately abundant, cooperative, diverse, and regenerative. Prosperity is not about struggling to get a result: it is about flowing towards a result. Flow is a truce with struggle, a cooperative effort, a sense of ease and grace. Flow is like a river that moves easily and effortlessly. Struggle is a blockage to the current that must be overcome. Blocks are like boulders, logs, or silt that block the flow. Struggle says we must push the current harder and more quickly to compensate for the blockage. Flow tells us to unblock the channel and restore the natural state of things. The only kind of flow that the scarcity game recognizes is cash flow. When money flows in so do all the good feelings, and when it flows out, so the good feelings flow out and bad feelings flow in. Scarcity and struggle are states of being, just like prosperity and flow. Struggle is a state of being that sees reality as a battlefield. This creates emotional states of anxiety, anger, and depression. Struggle is a state of ongoing tension. A person in a state of struggle will look tense and serious on the outside, and can be prickly and reactive. A person in a state of struggle looks out on to a hard and hostile world.

The Ancient Greek myth of Sisyphus is about struggle. Sisyphus upset the gods and was then condemned to roll a rock ceaselessly up a mountain. When he reached the top, the stone would fall back because of its own weight. The gods concluded that there is no more dreadful punishment than futile and hopeless labour. There is a lot of needless struggle in our world. Struggle can involve intense and pointless labour or it can come through a thousand and one lesser activities that keep us locked in futility and hopeless and unending effort.

Struggle does not believe in a world of love, support and abundance and so it creates a scarcity cage as a protection. 'Well,' the thinking goes, 'if the world is hostile then I need to protect myself, my possessions and my loved ones.' A close friend of mine has been talking about moving out of London and going to the coast. In one conversation, she spoke about her dream of leaving the busy city and living near the sea. Her partner, who worked in the city, was happy to support her dream. In another conversation she spoke about moving in terms of how difficult it would be, about how hard it would be to make new friends, and about whether they had enough resources for the transition. Nothing had changed externally; the only thing that had changed was her internal state. She was in a scarcity state and could not truly evaluate her situation. Her partner still supported the move but did not know how to deal with her sudden attack of doubt. When people are in scarcity states, they often want help but also resist accepting it. Another person was in a difficult financial situation. She asked people close to her for help but would then feel anxious, angry or depressed about the advice she received. She would withdraw from the people around her until she felt the urge to ask for advice again, and so the pattern continued.

For someone stuck in a scarcity state (such as anxiety, confusion, or rage) the kindest thing to do is either leave them alone or, if they are up for it, help them out. To help someone out of a scarcity state, the state itself needs to be interrupted. Interrupting a state is not like telling someone to snap out of it; this is likely to compound the state of feeling bad. Interrupting a scarcity state helps someone to break their habitual thinking and feeling and allows for something new to come through. It is a bit like changing gear in a car - before the shift can be made the gearbox has to pass through neutral. Interrupting a scarcity state can help put someone into a neutral space. This then allows them to choose more readily a more resourceful state such as curiosity, joy, or inspiration. There are many ways in which to interrupt a person's unresourceful state. Lovingly and powerfully speaking their name while they are talking is one method, using provocative humour another and saying or doing something unexpected yet another. A few years back, I was having dinner with the family of a friend. My friend's mother was becoming increasingly agitated and argumentative. As she continued arguing, I listened to catch what she was saying beneath her words. Then I took a chance and said to her, 'You know, you are obviously a very intelligent woman who just wants to be heard and respected.' She stopped and looked at me with a penetrating glance. The room fell silent for a few seconds that seemed to last an eternity. Then she lightened up and said, 'Yes, that is right.' Her state of aggression had been interrupted; the rest of the evening was considerably more enjoyable.

When someone is trapped in a scarcity state they will feel locked in a certain state of contraction. A person in a scarcity state will feel very strongly around issues of money. Money can become as important as the air that they breathe. They will feel that their very survival depends on money. People in scarcity states cannot make empowered choices. The scarcity state keeps our thoughts and feelings locked into a narrow bandwidth and then we respond habitually to life's challenges. Even when we know our responses will not produce the results we want, we will repeat them because we know no other way. The only way to change our results is to change our state from a contracted one to a more open and fluid one.

In Neuro Linguistic Programming, there is a saying that people have all the resources they need to succeed and to achieve their desired outcomes. In other words, there are no unresourceful people, only unresourceful states. People in an unresourceful state can be helped to return to a more resourceful one. In NLP, a resourceful state refers to any state in which a person can access internal abilities, emotions, memories, strategies and talents (either latent or already realized) and put them into some form of action. The state of flow is about dealing with the uncertainties of life from a strong centre. It is not about trying to control life or make it fit a pre-fixed pattern. This is a recipe for boredom and stuckness. A business consultant once told me that the biggest problem he encountered with many of his clients was dealing with their 'urge for premature certainty'. This leads to a quick-fix approach to challenges which often compounds problems. Flow is not about seeking to end a process too quickly but allowing the natural flow towards resolution to occur. Sometimes, we stay in the process too long and do not notice that we have left the flow.

Peter was in a well paid job but was bored. He held on to the job because he was uncertain of his next step in life and needed to feel secure. However, the longer he stayed, the more stuck he felt until he started to have minor disagreements with colleagues. This developed into major conflict over the space of the next couple of years. Because he lacked any real challenge in his work and was afraid to move on, he entered the struggle zone. The harder he struggled, the more painful it became until finally he got the message and resigned. Suddenly, he felt liberated. He had more time to do the things he wanted to do. After a period of rest, he found a new job that gave him a great sense of enjoyable challenge. He was back in the flow and every area of his life, from romance to friendship to travel, opened up.

Natalie was feeling very stuck and confused. She told me that she lived in a family in which she could not express her true feelings. Her father was very domineering and talked constantly, filling up all the space. To escape, Natalie began a romantic relationship only to find to her surprise and horror that the new boyfriend began to act like her father. She felt trapped but gathered up enough strength to end the relationship. She did not know how to deal with her father's dominating energy and was afraid of repeating the pattern in future relationships with men. We talked about the issue and she agreed to work on it through a ritual. We gathered a group of supportive friends to help her through the process. Together we worked on a basic format for the ritual without telling the group what was about to happen. Natalie was very nervous but decided that she had to face this issue and move beyond it. With the group around her in a circle, she began by putting on a mask and covering her mouth with some sticking tape to represent her inability to speak. She sat in front of two empty chairs representing her father and ex-boyfriend. She sat for a while in silence and then ripped off the mask and the tape over her mouth and started to express her true feelings. Soon, she was shouting and screaming and letting out years of suppressed emotions. When she had finished, she was held in silence by the group. When I saw her the next day, she looked radiant, happy and fully alive. She had returned to a flow state.

Ending a Scarcity State

The more intense a limiting state, the stronger the pattern-interrupt needs to be. To interrupt an unresourceful state you can:

Go for a walk; breathe more deeply; sit with a tree; listen to something humourous; write or paint; hit a pillow; do something playful;, speak out your own name forcefully; play some soothing, vigorous or uplifting music; speak gibberish for five minutes; have a friend do something unexpected; say an affirmation; drink some hot tea; recall a happy memory; read a poem; perform a simple ritual; do a vigorous physical activity; watch a movie; or just do something different – anything!

Prosperity = Entering the Flow

Mihaly Csikszentmihalyi is a psychology professor at the University of Chicago who has studied the lives of thousands of people for more than thirty years in search of what makes people's lives meaningful and satisfying. He has explored the lives of more than ninety of the world's most creative people – such as authors, painters and scientists – to find out how creativity has been a force in their lives. He has interviewed a number of painters to try and understand their concept of flow. He found that many artists could not tear themselves away from a painting once it started to get interesting. This state of fascination usually lasted until the picture was finished and then the artist would turn his or her attention to the next blank canvas. He discovered that flow was not so much about an end result as about a process. This contradicts the idea that human beings are motivated by results rather than the process itself. Artists are not the only ones who spend considerable time and effort in an activity that has few rewards outside itself. When we are growing up, we understand life through the art of play. We learn about life through having fun. You may have noticed that it is harder to learn about something you do not like. Adults enter the process of flow through play: it can be *Monopoly* or chess, athletics or hockey, gardening or playing the guitar. According to Mihaly Csikszentmihalyi, people who know how to play enter a mental state which he calls 'flow'. He used this term because this was the metaphor that many people gave him to describe their experiences. Flow tends to happen when we are actively involved in a difficult enterprise, in a task that stretches our mental and physical abilities. Apparently, any activity can result in flow: a game, a challenging job, anything that exercises our abilities to the utmost. Symptoms of flow include a narrowing of attention, a sense of being absorbed and a feeling of transcendence. There is a lessening of everyday concerns; the pianist does not think about hitting the wrong note nor does the rock-climber think about falling. There is a story about the Italian composer Rossini, who was composing an overture in bed one day because it was too cold to get up. Suddenly, his papers fell to the floor and scattered everywhere. Not wishing to break his creative flow, he simply started over again and wrote a brand new overture.

Flow is about a certain state that leads to certain experiences. For instance, it is not about *finding* the right partner: it is about *being* the right partner. It is not about *finding* wealth: it is about *feeling* wealthy. When we are in the right state, anything is possible. Happy people attract happy experiences. Wealthy people attract wealthy experiences. Generous people attract generous experiences. It is as the Buddha said long ago, 'There is no way to happiness. Happiness is the way.' Whatever we want, we must make it our discipline to embody. If we want success, we must get clear on how we would feel if we were successful and start embodying that state now. If we want serenity, we must act serenely. In time, it will become an habitual state and we will not have to work at it.

Flow, like life, is not just about a series of goals or outcomes, or a checklist of things to do. Flow is about all good things coming to us easily and effortlessly. One Valentine's Day, I decided at the last minute to go out on the town with my partner. We drove to a funky part of town and decided to experiment with going with the flow. We stood on the High Street and looked both ways; we both got an inner 'yes' to walk in a certain direction. After less than five minutes' walking, we passed an enticing looking Caribbean restaurant and felt that this was the place. We went inside. The atmosphere was breathtaking – the colour, the way the staff were dressed – we were in a world transported. We asked for a table and were told that all the tables had been booked a month in advance. Unperturbed, we continued on our adventure up the high street. Suddenly, a breathless waiter managed to catch up with us. He blurted out that somehow there was one table left; his manager had overheard the conversation and had checked and found that there had been a recent cancellation. We returned and had the meal of our lives.

Flow has been also called 'the zone' by many athletes, executives, musicians, and writers. It is a place where all thinking disappears; there is just a heightened knowing in the present. Here, miracles can happen, tournaments and contracts are won, and physical limits and creative boundaries are exceeded. It is an unpredictable place; you can never know when it will arise. There is no magic formula for entering 'the zone' but there are some magic ingredients. 'The zone' is not a literal place: it is a state of being where someone feels in a place of total balance, focus and involvement at all levels – mental, emotional and physical. In the film, *The Last Samurai,* Civil War hero Captain Nathan Algren, played by Tom Cruise, is a man adrift. He is enticed to Japan to train Japan's first modern conscript army. The enemy is the venerated Samurai, warriors who dedicate their lives to serving emperor and country. Algren is captured by the Samurai and finds himself in a very different cultural world. In one scene, he engages in a training fight, using wooden swords, with one of the Samurai sword masters. He loses each contest. But then one young Samurai whispers in his ear that he is thinking too much and worrying about what everyone else thinks. The next contest is very different. Captain Algren finds himself in a state of pure flow where, to everyone's surprise, he achieves a draw against his more experienced opponent.

Flow = A Meditation on Life

To enjoy high performance, it is important to be in a state of relaxed ease. This is a place of inner relaxation in which the senses feel fully alive and ready for instant action.

It is important to breathe. People who perform under pressure often speak about the importance of breathing. Stop and take some slow, deep breaths right down into the belly and then into the upper chest. Practise exhaling fully after each in-breath.

Embrace both great relaxation and tremendous focus at the same time. Be like a cat that can relax deeply and pounce in an instant.

Become so absorbed in your activity that it becomes a meditation.
Practise dancing, playing tennis, writing a story, or playing a musical
instrument and forget about everything except the activity itself. Flow
happens when there is no self-consciousness, when there is no
separation between the doer and the action. Flow happens when there
is only an awareness of the play itself.

Anchoring a Flow State

Take a resourceful state, such as confidence, calm, enthusiasm, or
serenity.
Be specific about how you want to feel.

Recall a particular time in your life when you felt that desired state.
Choose a powerful memory. Imagine yourself back in that experience
as if it is happening now. Notice what you see, hear what you were
hearing, feel what you were feeling in the moment. Feel the state that
you want in the present moment.

Choose a word and a body movement to anchor the feeling which
the memory has evoked. Be creative. For example, you can place your
left hand on your heart and say 'peace', or you can clench your right fist
and say 'strength', or touch your left thumb and index finger together
and whisper 'confidence'. Make the word and gesture as unique as
possible. Repeat as often as you need to create an anchor for the state.

Before any activity, simply set the required state by recalling the
memory and using the anchor. Using anchors will make a difference to
your internal state and to your effectiveness in the world. They can be
used before an interview or before a business meeting. You can also
anchor any of your goals or values with this technique. Simply work out
what feelings would be associated with achieving the goal or
embodying the value, find a suitable memory and voila!

Prosperity = The Flow of Giving

Prosperity is about generous giving and receiving whereas scarcity is
about taking and taking. Giving and receiving happen in the context of
relationships. Communities thrive and prosper when the flow of giving
and receiving happens between people. Whether it be the neighbour
who borrows a cup of sugar, the friend that hitches a lift to work or the
family that financially supports their children, communities create

prosperity. In the business community, giving and receiving is big business. For instance, on the Internet many people offer a whole range of freebies, including free downloadable software, and other informational files. Sometimes this leads to tremendous success. One company offered a freely downloadable computer program allowing PC users to talk to each other for free and make cut-price calls to mobiles and landlines. Since it was introduced in 2003, this free program has been downloaded more than 151 million times. In 2005, the online auction site eBay saw the potential of the product and bought Skype Technologies for $2.6 billion (£1.4 billion).[1]

If you think about it, has anything good ever come to you other than through a relationship of some kind? A boss may see the latent abilities in an employee and decide to mentor or promote them. A stranger can give a homeless person a gift of money, or make a donation to a good cause. A relative may leave money to someone they love in their will. There is no way in which money can flow to you except from another person. Therefore prosperity and flow have a lot to do with the quality of relationship. Many people focus on a lack of money as their core problem when the real issue is actually the quality of their relationship, firstly with themselves and then with others. The degree to which a person is really able to make a connection with another is the degree to which they are open to giving and receiving. This is the real basis for win/win scenarios.

Scarcity encourages a very different approach – a fierce kind of individualism that sees the world as a huge cake to be divided amongst the brave and industrious. When a community is filled with people looking out solely for their own self-interest, then it is no longer a community, it becomes just a group of people who hang out together occasionally. Scarcity is not interested in giving and receiving openly. It is concerned with conditional giving, taking and defending. It is about protecting the rights and profits of the few over the many. For instance, Jimmy Wales is the founder of Wikipedia, a charitable effort that organizes thousands of volunteers to write high quality encyclopaedia entries on the web in every language in the world. He is frequently frustrated by copyright limits on the free exchange of information and receives around two or three threatening communications from lawyers each week complaining of infringed copyright. He says 'copyrights have been repeatedly extended to absurd lengths'; this is the scarcity world of defending and taking. Scarcity is found wherever giving has conditions attached. This is the 'I'll scratch your back if you scratch mine' mentality. People who feel some kind of lack in their lives often give conditionally. For instance, in families the basic commodity of love is often given conditionally. This is the game of 'I will love you if you achieve, or please, or take care of me.' A Jewish friend of mine was being pressurized by her mother to marry someone who was Jewish. This was a problem for her since, at the time, she had a non-Jewish boyfriend. Finally, she said to her mother, 'I think sometimes that you only love me conditionally.' The mother replied, 'Of course I only love you conditionally!' Although a little shocking, at least she heard the truth direct from the horse's mouth. Most of us suspect that we are only loved conditionally but never get to hear it this clearly.

In Buddhism, three kinds of giving are recognized: beggarly giving, in which we give only once we have received; friendly giving, in which we are generous only to people who are generous in return; and royal giving, which is spontaneous and unconditional. There is so much royal giving in the world. For instance, The Random Acts of Kindness Foundation, established in the U.S. in 1995, helps people to spread kindness across the world. One couple in the UK began a company importing goods from Nepal and donating all the profits to helping orphans in that country. In a similar vein, the film of the book *Pay it Forward* (Pocket, 2003) by Catherine Ryan Hyde created the Pay It Forward Movement. The idea is that, by anonymously doing a favour for someone else, we are sowing seeds of generosity and kindness in another. That person will be inspired to do the same for another and so generosity spreads. Catherine Ryan Hyde says that she didn't expect a social movement to be born from her work but she has enjoyed watching it grow. The organization has a newsletter called 'Be Nice or Else'. Generosity is very much at work in the world; we just have to look for it.

There was an ordinary couple living in Brooklyn, USA. He was a professor of chemical engineering, with a small consulting business on the side and his wife was a former teacher who spent most of her time volunteering for New York civic and arts organizations. They had no children. When they died (he in 1995, she in 1998), it turned out that they were quite remarkable indeed for they had amassed a fortune through some very wise investing. All told, the couple bequeathed $340 million to several perennially cash-strapped Brooklyn institutions. Similarly in 2002, eBay co-founders Pierre Omidyar and Jeff Skoll, along with eBay Chief Executive Officer Meg Whitman, made combined donations to various charities of just over $99 million. In the same year, publishing magnate Walter Annenberg, bequeathed gifts worth nearly $1.4 billion, including about $1 billion in the estimated worth of his art collection, which he left to the Metropolitan Museum of Art in New York. In 2004 Bill and Melinda Gates gave away $3.35 billion and Susan Buffett, the wife of billionaire

Warren Buffett, left $2.55 billion in her will to help college scholarships and medical research.[2] As you can see, generosity is very much a part of our world.

Generous Giving

To be truly generous, we must first practise being generous with ourselves.

Do you give yourself the things that truly nourish you, such as enough time, space, rest, aloneness, silence, adventure, or beauty? If not, how about starting now?

Practise performing acts of senseless generosity to yourself. Buy yourself things that you love and enjoy. You do not need to spend much money each time – it could be as simple as buying yourself a tea in a beautiful café.

The next step is to practise being generous to others; perform one act of senseless generosity to someone else every day. You do not need to spend much money – it could be as simple as buying a tea for a homeless person or a flower for a stranger.

Prosperity = The Flow of Receiving

For over ten years, psychologist Richard Wiseman conducted a research project into luck.[3] He researched people who experienced persistent good or bad luck throughout their lives. He worked for several years with over a thousand volunteers, examining their personality differences on a number of different levels. His findings were revealing; he found that lucky people are more likely to achieve their dreams and ambitions because they think differently from unlucky people. They expect to be happy and successful and see bad luck as being short-lived. Lucky people tend to persevere in pursuit of their dreams or goals and can turn misfortune into good fortune. Lucky people tend to enjoy meeting and connecting with other people. They use body language that is attractive and inviting, and they smile and make eye contact more than unlucky people. They are more likely to initiate conversations and are more effective at 'building secure and long-lasting attachments'. They create a strong network of friendships and optimize their chances of a lucky encounter. Wiseman's research points towards luck being something that we generate ourselves.

Cheryl and her son Ian were on their way home when they passed by a young homeless man sitting on the side of the pavement. It was a very cold day and both Cheryl and her son wanted to give him some money. Cheryl only had 60p in her purse and gave it anyway. They walked on and wondered if they should buy the young man a tea from a local coffee shop. They went to a cash point, withdrew some money and then bought the young man an expensive chai latte and a nice cake. They hurried back but the man was not there any more. Disappointed, they walked on, hoping to find someone who would receive the gift. A few minutes down the road, they saw another homeless man and they asked him if he would like a hot drink and a cake. He happily received the gifts. Cheryl said afterwards, 'It was nice to see him receiving them.' Cheryl and her son walked away feeling that the gift had been well received.

Jennifer wanted to go to the Live8 concert. This was the concert that was put together to help make poverty history. She emailed all the people she knew to see if anyone had a spare ticket. She checked the websites, and searched Google but had no luck. The concert was sold out. On the day of the concert she got dressed and gathered all the cash she had and off she went. As she walked from Victoria to Hyde Park Corner she walked past a ticket tout and she asked him how much. But the price was way beyond her means. She walked through the underpass and emerged outside the gates where there were so many people – many of them carrying signs saying, 'I need 1 ticket'. She walked passed them and found a place to look through the fence. She had been standing there no more than 15 seconds when a voice next to her said, 'Do you have a ticket?'

'No,' she replied, turning towards the man.

'Do you want one?'

'Yes,' she said, 'How much?'

'Nothing. It's for charity. It felt wrong to sell it so I thought I'd turn up and see who looked like they really wanted it.' Jennifer was in the flow of receiving.

Alex fell in love with Bali and decided to open a business in London selling Balinese art and furniture. Although the shop was in a good position and it was filled with beautiful things that were reasonably priced, his business failed. Another shop sold products from Bali that were more expensively priced. This shop was in a far less prominent position yet it continued to do very well. Although Alex loved the things he sold he did not love doing business. The second shop was more inviting and pleasurable to visit. Alex's business failed because he did not know how to receive customers.

John had a small business selling precious jewellery from New Zealand. Within fifteen minutes of meeting him, he had told me his journey of the last few years. He was half Italian and half Native American Indian. He arrived in England four years ago with several hundred pounds. Shortly afterwards, he started selling Maori jewellery in a London market. Now he runs a very financially successful business. If you were to meet him, you would understand why he is so successful. He has an amazing ability to connect with people, and he is an incredible storyteller. He speaks about the craftsmen who made the jewellery, about the Maori legends they relate to, and the gifts that each piece offers the owner. When I left him, I had bought an expensive piece and to this day I have never regretted the purchase. I wear the stone often. I came away with a beautiful Maori jewellery piece and also a great story that continues to inspire me in my more melancholy moments.

Joseph Pulitzer became the owner of one of the largest newspapers in the U.S. He was also a generous philanthropist despite originally being a penniless teenage immigrant from Hungary. At first, he found it hard to find employment so he spent a great deal of time playing chess in the local library. On one of his visits, he met an editor of a local newspaper and was offered a job. Eventually, he became the editor of the paper and then its owner. His entire career began with a chance encounter in a library. Lucky people tend to be in the right place at the right time. They are open to receive from the unlikeliest of sources. My young stepson and his friends came across an old sofa dumped on the street. He decided that the sofa would make a good trampoline and began jumping up and down on it. Unexpectedly, 420 euros suddenly popped out as he jumped. Although a note was put on the sofa, no-one claimed the money and the friends all shared equally in the windfall. Good fortune made each of them 70 euros the richer.

Fiona is a practitioner of generous giving and is sometimes in the fortunate position of being able to give away some amazing personal and professional development trainings for free. On one occasion, she offered a friend one of these trainings. Now, this training course normally costs around £2,500 and it was a fantastic offer. When she made the offer her friend went very quiet. Even though they had known each other for a couple of years, Fiona could almost hear her friend thinking, 'I know Fiona, yet no-one gives away a course this expensive for free; where's the catch?' Because the scarcity game bombards us with special offers and other enticements to hook us into some deal or another, it is little wonder that some people look a gift horse in the mouth. Fiona did manage to find several friends who were open to receive and they were all immensely grateful for the experience.

The state of receiving is not about having expectations or demands. These are huge barriers to real receiving. Asking is one thing; it is a great skill to develop. Some people are amazing in asking for what they need and want. Demanding is something else; the difference between the two is shown when a request is refused. A person who asks will accept the 'no' and move on. A person who demands will get very upset at being refused. Hidden expectations and demands are a cause of great pain. When expectations are not met, disappointment, frustration and even outright anger are often the result.

Expectations and demands are often hidden. Imagine meeting someone very attractive; you make eye contact, you exchange a few words, and the person then looks at you and asks you out for a date. They look genuine and, just as you are about to say 'yes', they tell you that you must accept because they feel lonely and also they have not been to a great restaurant for ages. They tell you that if you accept, it would be really nice because they are working on some deep issues with their father or mother at the moment and know you are the perfect candidate to help them out right now. They end by saying that you need to pick them up at 8pm and they hand you a list of their top ten favourite restaurants. By now, the prospect of going out on the date may look less attractive. In real life, expectations and demands are rarely expressed so overtly. If they were, there would probably be far less disappointment, suffering and heartbreak in the world.

It can come as a shock to some people to hear that other people were not put on this earth to fulfil our spoken and unspoken expectations. To the degree that we have expectation, so will other people resist giving to us from the heart. Receiving is like standing on a street corner collecting for a good cause, knowing that people will contribute. And they do. Expectation is like standing on a street corner collecting for a good cause, wondering who is going to give money, getting upset when people who should contribute do not, and wondering what other people will think about the amount collected at the end of the day.

Expectations and demands are not the only block that prevents real receiving. The following story illustrates an interesting point about receiving. Carol had parents who were strongly directive. As she was growing up, they chose everything for her. She was a fashion conscious teenager, yet she was not able to choose clothes for herself. Her parents were also strongly influential in what she studied at school. When her teachers told her parents that she had great artistic abilities and recommended that she study art, her parents made her study foreign languages instead. As an adult, they even bought an expensive flat for her. It was a fantastic flat but since they gave her no choice in the matter she still felt furious and disempowered. She could not really appreciate the gift because she had no choice in the matter. Some years later, her partner bought her a beautiful handmade coat. He knew she would love the coat because she had seen the design some weeks before and immediately fell in love with it. But she could not receive the coat and wanted to take it back. In the store, her partner watched in amazement as she tried on every coat on display. Finally, she came back to the coat her partner had originally bought for her and said, 'I choose this one.' Her partner laughingly asked why she needed to try on every other coat before choosing the one he had originally bought for her. She explained that since her parents had always chosen everything for her as she was growing up, she needed to make the choice her own. She looked proudly at the coat and said, 'I have chosen the coat and now it is mine.'

Some people are good at giving away training courses, others are good at giving away money, and others precious gifts. Some people are good at receiving love and appreciation. Others are good at receiving opportunities. You may have heard the saying 'what goes around comes around'. People who give away books find that they always have more books than they need. People who give away clothes find that they always have more clothes than they know what to do with. It seems to be a principle in life that what we give away with love returns to us lovingly. What we throw away with disdain or regret will someday return in the same manner. Some people dump their romantic partners because they do not like something about them and find further down the line that it happens again or, the reverse, they are dumped in the same way. The important thing to note here is that it is not just about giving away more stuff in order to receive more stuff. The more we can let go the more we can experience being in the flow of all good things returning to us. The more we release those good things to other people the more they can flow around and touch many more.

What do you most want in life? Whatever it is, you must find out how to give it away and then it will start to flow back to you. If you want friendship, you must be a friend to others. If you want love and appreciation, you must start to love and appreciate others with no expectation of it being given to you back by the same people. If you want people to be more generous to you, you must become more generous. How about smiling at people? In some areas this might feel like physically assaulting another but give it a go anyhow. How about making one good thing happen to another person every day? In no time you will find that you are magnetic to good things.

Blocks to Receiving

Many forms of inner resistance can become blocks to receiving. However, the most common blocks are:
  Having overprotective or controlling parents;
  Focusing on the needs of others at the expense of our own needs;
  Not knowing what we really want;
  Being attached to certain results;
  Being a compulsive giver;
  Being a compulsive competitor;
  Feeling unloved or undeserving;
  Feeling guilt or believing that we are not good enough;
  Believing that good things must be fought for and taken;
  Believing that receiving only comes as the result of hard work;
  Believing that life gives with one hand and takes with the other;
  Feeling shame, leading to our feeling flawed and inferior to other people;
  Fear of intimacy and thus keeping people at a distance;
  Issues of social justice – because others suffer, so must we;
  Distrusting people's motives for giving;
  Feeling that gifts come with strings or conditions attached.

Opening to Receive

Receiving is allowing good things to come easily and gracefully. It is based on the qualities of faith, openness, and trust.
  Receivers are open channels and abundance flows to them and through them:
  They are generous in their receiving and say 'thank you';
  They honour the gifts that others wish to bestow upon them;
  They know their needs and feel that they deserve the best in life;
  They do not place modest limits on their ability to receive;
  They feel love and appreciation for the generosity of others;
  They do not limit the ways in which good things can come to them;
  They believe in their good fortune;
  They believe that the universe gives with both hands;

They feel comfortable with intimacy;

They say ' yes' to life; they do not say 'yes' to one good thing and 'no' to another;

They see people suffering but receive in order to be able to give more;

They trust people's core motives for giving;

They believe in grace;

They are not attached to the details of who will give to them, and what and how they give.

Just Say 'Thank You!'

'Thank you' is a great gateway to receiving. Whenever you receive a gift from another, whether that be a smile or a moment of humour or a more tangible sort of gift, remember to thank the person. Even if you cannot directly say it, express it in some other way or just silently send them a 'thank you' thought. What we appreciate increases in our lives.

References

1. http://news.bbc.co.uk/1/hi/business/4237338.stm
2. http://sanjose.bizjournals.com/sanjose/stories/2003/02/17/daily72.html
   http://service.spiegel.de/cache/international/spiegel/0,1518,407036-2,00.html
3. The Luck Factor, Arrow, 2001

Chapter 9

Prosperity = Radical Aliveness

---

*The sunbeam sparkles only in the sunlight and the
ripples dances as it rests upon the ocean. Yet in neither
sun nor ocean is the power that rests in you.*

A COURSE IN MIRACLES

There was once a monk who sat meditating alone in a high cave on a lonely mountain. He remained there for forty years. He owned nothing and wanted nothing. He ate next to nothing and drank only water. Over time, his meditation practice gave him great insight and many supernatural abilities. He could remember and recite any sacred scripture. He had developed the power to control his body and emotions and could endure great pain for many hours. Yet, in spite of all these years of spiritual practice and accomplishment, he remained miserable. His spiritual retreat was an escape from life, rather than an embracing of it. He had not managed to learn the essential and practical skill of living happily with himself and others.

Principle Nine   *Aliveness, inspiration and passion are the signs
                    that point to inner prosperity. Feedback points the
                    way to success and prosperity in the world.*

Prosperity = Aliveness, Inspiration and Passion

Aliveness, inspiration and passion are prosperity states. They lead to action, which means getting our hands a little dirty in the soil of life. Prosperity is about feeling fully alive and engaged in the world of action. It is one thing to read about life and another to get out into the world and learn through experience. The gardener can never know the joy of planting and watching living things grow and flower just by reading about it. It is through action that we feel fully alive. Without taking action not very much can happen in the garden of our life.

The mythologist Joseph Campbell used to advise people to follow their bliss, meaning to follow their sense of aliveness, passion and wonder. Passion is a fiery quality; it can ignite in a moment and burn for just a few minutes or a whole lifetime. Following our bliss is very different from following the highest paying opportunity, or from taking the job that looks good on paper. Aliveness and passion do not ignite in the head: they ignite within the whole body. Have you ever spoken to someone who was on fire with enthusiasm and passion? You may have found that you felt like walking away or else you felt enlivened by their passion. Passionate people are the movers and shapers of the world. They get things done because they are highly motivated and because they inspire others.

One of my favourite films of all time is *Jerry Maguire*. In the film, Tom Cruise plays Jerry Maguire, a sports agent willing to do just about anything to get the biggest possible contract for his clients plus the biggest commission for himself. Then one day Jerry has an attack of conscience after seeing one of his sports stars lying in hospital surrounded by his loving family. Because of this he is inspired to write a mission statement for his company and proposes to the partners of the firm that the company take a more caring and ethical approach to their business. When he goes into work the next day his fellow workers applaud him as a hero. However the company, that is only really interested in making more profit, fires him at the first opportunity. Determined to follow his heart, he sets up his own business with the help of Dorothy, another employee of the money grabbing firm who leaves because she is inspired by his vision. There are many magical moments in the film. In one such moment Jerry is having a telephone conversation with his one remaining client, Rod Tidwell, a self-centred Black American Soccer player. Jerry has to convince him to believe in him and retain him as his agent. To do so, Rod asks Jerry to shout down the phone the mantra, 'Show me the money'. He does this and convinces Rod to stay. Passion is what drives Jerry through all his challenges to eventual success.

Inspiration is a prosperity state. It was inspiration that drove the Greek mathematician Archimedes to leap naked from his bath and run down the street shouting '*Eureka*', the Greek word for 'I've found it'. Inspiration can come in such a moment. Joseph Campbell found his passion for storytelling when he was seven years old on the day his father took him to see Buffalo Bill's Wild West show. As a child, Samuel Langhorne

Clemens, alias Mark Twain, drew inspiration from watching steamboats passing along the Mississippi River. The singer Johnny Cash grew up in a house by a railway track in Arkansas. Later, he just loved to sing about trains. His father, a depression era cotton farmer, used to ride the freights in search of work when there wasn't any cotton to pick. In the early 1960s, Johnny Cash made two albums called *Ride this Train* and *All Aboard the Blue Train*. Perhaps one of the most inspiring things I have heard is the true story of Jean-Dominique Bauby who, at the age of 43, suffered a massive stroke that left him almost completely paralyzed, unable to move except for his left eyelid. There was no hope of significant recovery. Although his body was immobilized, he dictated a book of his experiences by blinking his eyelid to an assistant who used a specially devised alphabet. Bauby survived just long enough to see his book, *The Diving Bell and the Butterfly,* published.[1] It sold 150,000 copies in the first week of its publication. According to the Oxford dictionary, inspiration can be a sudden brilliant idea, a source of inspiring influence, and the state of being stimulated into a creative activity. The word 'inspiration' derives from the Latin *spirare* which means 'to breathe'.

Sometimes things are birthed with great inspiration and passion and then the initial spark goes out. Sometimes a business is created with a combination of great tenacity and inspiration and then, once it is established, consolidation and continuing profit become the most important things. Passion needs to be nurtured or it will not endure. Passion needs to be fed with inspiration on a daily basis. Passion is like a pet that needs to be loved every day, not now and then. Many things can block inspiration, such as cynicism, hatred, hypocrisy, humiliation, prejudice, rejection, restriction, or routine.

Degas grew up in a wealthy family and was able to fully indulge his love of painting. When he hit sixty, he looked back on his life and concluded that his work had been a waste of time. He retreated to his studio determined to re-inspire himself and create something radically different. For the next twenty years, he devoted himself to producing some of his greatest masterpieces. Sometimes inspiration needs a period of stillness or incubation to spark into life.

Everyone has a sense of passion; in some of us it is buried a little more deeply than in the rest. Sometimes, surface passions present themselves and seem to be the thing to follow when really they are merely pointers to something deeper. A client, Alice, came to me feeling uncertain about her life direction and wanted some help in getting clearer. We talked for a while about her passion for literature and ideas, yet beneath this I sensed that a deeper passion was waiting to be voiced. Suddenly, the conversation shifted and she began speaking about wanting a child. Work shifted into the background and we spent the next hour talking about motherhood. Tears came to her eyes as she talked about her passion for having a child. It was little wonder that she was unclear about work when what she really wanted was to get down to the core business of being a mother.

Sometimes we feel stuck because we are focusing on things we have little passion for. John hated being a shop assistant. He wanted to do something different but was so consumed with resentment that he had little space to feel passionate about very much else. Then a friend told him that he would stay stuck unless he could see the good in what he was doing. Although he felt sceptical at first, he began to see that the thing that he liked the most was talking to people. He liked to know what made them tick, not just what things they wanted to buy. He decided to play a little and just chat to people for the pleasure of it. Not only did people respond well but soon his sales record went up. The more he focused on the things that inspired him, the easier and more free he felt. In time, he left the job and found a new one where his people skills were well rewarded.

Passion is the compass that can guide us through the labyrinth of suffering and stress to a different landscape. Our heart knows they way whilst our head can only make its most informed guess. When we combine our passion with the insight of the intellect, we move more swiftly in the direction of our life calling. Donna had a passion for beauty and creativity. She decided to explore these qualities through jewellery making. She kept at it for three years but found that it did not feed another need of hers for real connection with people. She spent long hours making intricate pieces but this meant that she had to concentrate in silence on what she was doing. Eventually, she gave up and tried something else. She started to write; not only did her passion ignite but she found a way to connect with people meaningfully. She started interviewing others to find out about their stories which she then lovingly shaped into beautiful pieces. She is now a very successful writer.

Inspiration is something we must breathe in daily if we are to build up enough steam to leave the gravitational field of the old scarcity game. Inspiration is cultivated and grown in environments of caring, congruence, connection, creativity, fairness, forgiveness, freedom, healing, hope, and openness.

Inspiration unlocks our natural gifts and talents, which are essential if we are to live a prosperous life. Inspiration does not require lots of money; in fact, quite the opposite. Marcel Bich had a chance encounter with a wheelbarrow that gave him the idea for the ball point pen. In 2005, the French BIC Corporation sold its 100 billionth pen. Alex, an ordinary middle class graduate living in messy student digs in Nottingham was different from most other students. What made him different was that he was on his way to making his first million before the age of 21. He came up with a simple idea that set the internet alight. He created a website called 'The Million Dollar Homepage' which contained exactly one million pixels. Pixels are the tiny dots that make the images on a computer screen. He set the site up and sold space to advertisers for $1 a pixel. The website captured the imagination of advertisers and was so successful that in the first month alone Alex sold more than 300,000 pixels at $1 each.[2]

Cirque du Soleil, a motley troupe of jugglers, acrobats, stiltwalkers and musicians put on a show in 1982 to help celebrate Canada's 450th anniversary. Because they had little money, the troupe had to rely on originality and theatrical innovation. Through using outrageous costumes, original music, and clever performers it was a rousing success. The show combined the best of circus and theatre, and thus began to attract bigger and bigger audiences. Cirque du Soleil is now a multi-million dollar business whose shows have been seen by over 37 million people all over the world.[3]

The unlikely French musical *Les Miserables* was written in an attempt to embrace deeply unfashionable issues on stage – revolution, ideology, suffering, struggle and redemption. The co-writers were virtually unknown and had little experience in writing a traditional musical. Yet, in 2005, on its 20th anniversary the total box office sales for the show worldwide amounted to a staggering £1.25 billion. Boublil commented on his success, 'I was just trying to write something that I liked.'[4]

In 1934, at the height of the Great Depression, Charles Darrow, who was unemployed, took to designing a board game. He produced some game sets with the help of a friend who was a printer and sold 5,000 units to a local department store. In its first year of sales in 1935, *Monopoly* was the best-selling game in America. To-date over 200 million games have been sold worldwide.[5]

Ignite Your Inspiration

What kinds of people inspire you? Is it creative, expressive, courageous, poetic, or eccentric kinds of people?

Look for inspiration everywhere – in books, films, TV shows, and in the situations and people you encounter.

Start doing some activities that inspire you. If you are inspired by creative people then do something creative; if you are inspired by music, start to perform music in some way.

Make a practice of reading and seeing inspiring things.

Sit in silence and contemplate all the things for which you have a passion. When you think about different things they will evoke a different response in your emotions and body. Passion is a radical aliveness in the body. It makes us want to jump and dance around.

It is no coincidence that some of the most highly paid people in the world are in the business of inspiring others – namely film stars, performers, musicians, and singers. Take the inspirational Oprah Winfrey, who has touched the hearts of millions; she has entertained, enlightened and uplifted millions of viewers for the past two decades. She runs a monthly women's lifestyle magazine with a circulation of 2.6 million readers each month. Through her private charity, The Oprah Winfrey Foundation, she has helped to empower women, children and families in the U.S. and around the world. It has directed millions of dollars towards providing a better education for students who have great merit but little means. She also has developed schools to educate thousands of children internationally. Her public charity *Oprah's Angel Network* has raised millions for non-profit organizations across the globe. Inspiration is big business. Richard Olivier, the son of the late Laurence Olivier, uses the inspiration of Shakespeare to teach business executives about things like leadership. He draws upon 'Henry V' to show how a true leader inspires his or her followers and achieves victory in the face of overwhelming odds. Simon Woodroffe, the inspiration behind Yo Sushi, brought inspiration across from the entertainment world into the business world with tremendous success. Following a £10 million buy-out, Simon now spends much of his time being a motivational speaker to corporate audiences. Richard Branson forged Virgin, an amazingly inspirational, innovative and successful business. Virgin is based on being unique as well as having practical values such as wishing to provide good value for money and a high quality service. Orange began building a strong, fresh, clear identity in 1994 that set it apart in a telecoms market filled with high-tech jargon. Its message, 'The future's bright, the future's Orange' was a revolution in the making. In 1996, with a valuation of £2.4 billion, Orange plc became the youngest company to enter the FTSE-100.[6]

There is perhaps no quality needed more in the world of politics than inspiration. Great inspirational leaders have the capacity to lead nations through terrible trials. From Alexander the Great to Winston Churchill, inspiration has shaped history. In 1863, after the terrible slaughter at the battle of Gettysburg, Abraham Lincoln managed to rally the nation through his inspirational Gettysburg address. During the latter part of the 20th century, Mikhail Gorbachev inspired the common people of the Soviet Union with his principles of *glasnost* (openness) and *perestroika* (change). He ended the war in Afghanistan, ended communist rule in Eastern Europe, brought freedom of speech to the Soviet citizens and led the way to two broad disarmament pacts that brought the world out of the Cold War. Through his inspirational determination, vision and courage, he had made the world a safer place. Similarly, Nelson Mandela steered South Africa towards freedom and justice despite great opposition, prejudice and oppression. Could you imagine how prosperous our world would be if all our politicians were so inspiring? Would such an inspired world waste billions on warfare or allow cut-throat capitalism to suck the life blood out of both the earth and its people?

Prosperity = Action and Feedback

There is an old Sufi story that tells of four towns. In each town, people were starving to death. Each town had a bag of seeds. In the first town, no one knew how to plant them. Everyone starved. In the second town, one person knew how to plant them but did nothing about it. Everyone starved. In the third town, one person knew about seeds. He proposed to plant them in exchange for being declared king. All ate, but were ruled. In the fourth town, one person knew what seeds were and how to plant them. He not only planted the seeds, but taught everyone the art of gardening. All ate, and all were free and empowered.

In life, we can either do nothing and let things stay the same or we can do something and things can get either better or worse. Reality tends to feel worse when a poor idea is first conceived, then believed in and then acted upon. Sometimes, a poor idea when acted upon can bring short term gains but, in the long run, it will bring diminishing results. Take an extreme example, such as Hitler, who had the idea of liberating Germany. He sought to do this by invading neighbouring countries in Europe. Initially, this action brought a certain amount of success in that Germany's sphere of economic and military power was extended, however, in the long run, it led to the utter destruction of Germany.

Reality tends to feel better when a good idea is conceived, then believed in and then put into action. Sometimes a great idea is not recognized or does not take hold immediately but, in the long run, it leads to extraordinary results. Take the example of Gandhi: he had the idea of liberating India, and he sought to do this through non-violent demonstration. Initially, this idea brought a strong reaction from the British authorities who naturally did not like it very much at all. In the long run, India was liberated from British rule.

Every action has consequences. Doing nothing also has consequences. Every action gives results which tell us how to proceed. Some actions are worth repeating, others need adjusting and others discarding. The most powerful lessons in life come from our actions, not through thinking about action. Action gives various forms of feedback. We are always receiving feedback if only we have the eyes to see and the ears to listen. A friend of mine had a father and an uncle who both shared a passion for boats. His father made fabulous wooden model boats with an extraordinary amount of detail. However, his uncle who owned his own business set aside a portion of his manufacturing plant to construct his own boat. Although it took him around twenty years to finish, he did get it into water and eventually sailed it. I asked my friend what the difference was between the two men. He replied that his uncle was entrepreneurial and that his father was simply averse to taking risks. Feedback comes through action. If we are not willing to take action in pursuit of our dreams, we limit the amount of feedback that we will receive from the world.

Feedback is an integral part of learning and understanding. Often, the kind of feedback people get when learning something is along the lines of, 'you're not doing it very well', or 'you must do better next time', or 'that's not bad'. Most of us have passed through an education system that marks our efforts on a scale from 1 to 100. We have been conditioned to notice where we have gone wrong rather than where we have done something well. For instance, some years ago I ran a two hour workshop; at the end, the group gave feedback on the evening. All of the feedback was consistently good and useful except for that of one person who made a number of very critical and not very helpful comments. You can imagine the feedback I still remember years later. We have been brought up with the idea that negative feedback is more useful than positive feedback. Isadora's mother was a theatrical director. Isadora grew up loving the theatre and went to drama school. Although a talented actress, her mother was always critical of her performances and she grew up believing that critical feedback was more useful and more credible than praise and appreciation. This resulted in a kind of glass ceiling on her ability to break into higher levels of success. Fortunately for both her peace of mind and her career she has opened to receive more positive feedback.

To be useful, feedback needs to be specific, and help us to move in the direction in which we want to go. The more specific the feedback, the more useful it is. I heard a dramatic example of the use of such feedback from a friend. It was set in a coaching seminar where the facilitator asked for a volunteer from the participants. One person volunteered and he was asked to sit with his back to the audience. The facilitator put a waste paper bin some yards behind him and gave him some tennis balls. He then asked the volunteer to throw the balls one by one over his shoulder and try and get the balls in the bin. The volunteer tried and missed on several occasions. The facilitator then said that the audience would help by giving feedback. The audience, who were primed for the next bit, started criticizing the ball thrower each time he missed by saying things like 'terrible', 'useless' and 'missing by miles'. The ball thrower did not get any better; if anything, he was getting worse. The facilitator then asked the volunteer ball thrower if he would like any different feedback. The volunteer thought about it for a moment and then said that what he would like was specific feedback on how far he was missing the target. Specifically he wanted to know how far to the left or right and how far in front or behind. The volunteer then used this feedback to have a ball on target within three throws.

In 1854, when Florence Nightingale heard about the terrible conditions and suffering in the Crimean War, she led a party of nurses there to help out. Although known as the 'Lady of the Lamp' by the soldiers she nursed, she was more like the 'Lady of the Iron Fist'. She was not only a great administrator and promoter of change but one of the earliest pioneers of the use of statistics. She once commented that she found statistics 'more enlightening than a novel'. She loved to bite on hard facts and, under her regime of care in the Crimea, the death rate fell from 42% to 2.2%. There was little arguing with this kind of feedback.

Feedback is valuable information which we ignore at our peril. Many people and organizations waste a considerable amount of time, energy and money when they misidentify a problem and then apply an incorrect solution. Using feedback helps to avoid this common mistake. One organization had a problem of poor morale amongst the staff, which led to decreasing profitability. The solution adopted by the organization was to introduce a new, costly and complicated IT system. It did nothing for falling morale and made a bigger dent in the organization's finances. No-one had ever asked the staff how they felt. One day someone did and they heard some interesting feedback. They also heard some interesting solutions. A consultant friend of mine often faces this kind of problem in the organizations in which he works. He has been called into organizations to deliver various training programs and, when he asks the question, 'What makes this the right solution?' and the answer is, 'because the staff are demoralized and under-performing', his standard reply is, 'Did you hire them that way?'. If we listen to what people are really telling we can then understand the real problem and so we are less likely to waste both time and money chasing the wrong solution.

There are many different sources of feedback. Even a person's body-language gives valuable feedback. In a training seminar, I once witnessed a process between two people where I was the observer. One person had to identify an issue or problem which they wanted to move beyond. The second person was there to help facilitate the process. The issue she raised involved her work and whether to stay working part time or resign and find another job. As she spoke of each option, her body language and tone of voice altered. When she spoke about one particular option, her eyes became more sparkly, she smiled more and she became more animated and pointed excitably with her fore finger. Finally, she worked out the best solution. As you may have guessed, it was the one where she became more animated and sparkly. Anyone watching from the outside, without knowing the issue or the possible solutions, would have been able to work out the best option to take by reading her body language.

To use feedback, it is important not only to start being actively engaged in looking out for it, but also to start asking for it. In NLP, there is the saying that 'there is no failure, only feedback'. What is often classified as failure is really just information and feedback that can be used either to beat oneself over the head or to plan future actions, endeavours, and projects. In the story of the person throwing tennis balls over his shoulder, each failure could be used as an excuse to criticize or to give valuable information to allow him to get closer to the target. Every miss paved the way for a future hit. Everything is information that can be used either for our growth or for our diminishment.

Using Feedback as a Compass

Choose something that you want to do more of and be better at. Let us take the example of wanting to be a better public speaker.

Adopt an attitude of curiosity about this issue, a desire to know how to do it better. Start collecting feedback; ask your friends to listen to your speaking and to tell you what they felt you did well and what they felt could be improved and how. You could also record yourself or stand in front of a mirror and then give yourself feedback.

Then ask for feedback from other people. What do they have to say about your delivery, pace, tone of voice, intonation, content etc?
Collate all the feedback.
What are the common themes or issues?
Which areas need adjusting and which are fine?
Which internal or external resources are needed to improve the results?

Adjust your performance and collect feedback from yourself and from others once more. Has anything changed?
Are you nearer or further away from where you want to go?
Continue until you reach the level of skill that you desire.

In the scarcity game, the kind of feedback used most frequently is, 'how much money am I getting?' or 'how much do I own?' or 'how profitable is this company?' In the prosperity game, money is just one of many forms of feedback.

Prosperity is concerned with entering into an inner state of fulfilment and happiness. Prosperity is also interested in creating meaningful results in the world. A couple that I have known for some years decided to move because they were receiving certain feedback from their existing house. They told me it was 'as if the house just started to wear out'. Not only were things tangibly going wrong (like the plumbing), they were also receiving a certain kind of feedback from their neighbours, one of whom started to complain about the number of cars parked outside their house. This was the final straw. They were astonished to find that their house had so risen in value that they were able to buy a cheaper house of the same size a short distance away. It enabled them to pay off the whole of their mortgage and still have £50,000 in the bank.

Feedback around something like money is fairly easy to gauge. It is usually clear whether someone is doing well financially or not. One young woman was not doing well in her business. She decided to stick her head in the sand and persevere no matter what the financial feedback. One day she was encouraged to really look at the figures. It was as clear as day that something was not working. She said to me later 'my bank statement really started to speak to me.' She used the feedback to make adjustments to what she was doing in the world. In time she started to see much better financial results.

For feedback to be effective, it should be something tangible that we can measure objectively rather than a feeling around something. Feelings are a form of feedback. Yet people often use their feelings to deny objective reality. It is hard to measure how much our overall quota of happiness has increased over a certain period of time. Feelings flow and change in a way that objective facts do not. We may feel good about something at one moment and not so good at another. A bank statement gives a certain amount of tangible feedback. Receiving five job interviews in one month is tangible and useful feedback. Feedback is information from the objective world that tells us how we are doing in relation to it.

Feedback helps us adjust our trajectory through life. Feedback helps someone who is not doing well to do better. Feedback also helps a person who is successful replicate that success elsewhere. Feedback can help us discover our winning formula.

During the 1992 U.S. presidential campaign, Clinton was not doing very well. His speeches tried to touch on everything and had no real focus. Then his campaign manager suddenly had a flash of intuition – the economy was the core issue to focus on. From that moment on, the campaign turned around and in every speech Clinton hammered home the importance of getting the economy in order. He won the election. There was no arguing with this kind of feedback.

Prosperity = Powerful Actions

For action to be successful, it must be carried out with 100% intention behind it. Nothing less will bring success. If we are doing something at 50%, only half of our intention is present and half is somewhere else, perhaps pulling in the opposite direction. If we are doing something at 99% we are a lot closer but there is a vast gap between 99% and 100%. We can only appreciate this when we do something with 100% effort and intention. At this level, we become irresistible and nothing can stop us from achieving the results we want. Strong actions are statements of our determination and resolve. The world responds to clear and decisive actions. There have been many innovative ideas that were not followed through: Xerox invented the mouse, icons and windows but it was Apple that first made them a reality in the world. The quartz powered digital watch was invented in Switzerland but the Japanese were the first to really invest in it. The business world is filled with planners and inventors who waited too long.

Powerful actions are statements about who we are becoming. Action is a vehicle for personal change. The way to get somewhere is to embody the steps of being there. If we feel we lack confidence, one way to become more confident is to act confidently. What might begin as a performance can soon change into the real thing. People scared of singing in public do not have to stop being scared before they sing. The act of singing itself breaks through the fear and activates a greater sense of confidence. If you want to be wealthy, start acting wealthily. One friend wanted to live in a large and beautiful house. She decided to do something to affirm her wealth and bought an expensive coffee percolator; each time she drank a cup of coffee she was reminded of living in her beautiful house. Another young woman was worried about money. She decided to take a big step by giving a friend the £500 she needed to pay for a personal development seminar. This act of generosity helped her to break through to a new level of personal generosity. Coincidentally, she not only felt a lot better about herself but soon afterwards received an unexpected gift worth several times the amount she had originally given.

Actions are statements to the world of our choices. Successful people make it a habit to make successful choices. Unhappy people have made a number of choices towards being unhappy, until it becomes habitual. Everyday we need to choose the things we desire. If we want love, we need to choose it everyday. If we want self-belief, we must make choices that support it everyday. Choice is something that atrophies unless it is used. It is important to keep choosing the things that are working and keep choosing to let go of the things that are not working.

Actions are statements of either the win-lose or win-win principle. Win-win says that real success and happiness result from a co-operative effort with others. This is an alien concept in the scarcity game. Steven Covey wrote about win-win situations in his international best-seller, *The Seven Habits of Highly Effective People* (Simon & Schuster, 1990). Win-win is based on the assumption that there is plenty for everyone. This is different from the competitive win-lose situation that is really a paradigm where everyone loses. Win-win is based on mutually beneficial agreements and solutions, and shared resources, not on getting one's way through the use of position, status, or sheer force of will. Win-win is based on the idea that synergy is a better way to operate than competition.

Synergy is the principle that the whole is greater than the sum of its parts. The word comes from the Ancient Greek *sun* and *ergos,* meaning to work together. Nature works with the principle of synergy. Human synergy happens when people help each other out. All communities know the value of win-win action. For example, if one person is too short to reach an apple on a tree, he could sit on the shoulders of another person to pluck the apple. They could then share the fruit between them. Communities are prosperous because they can pool resources, information, ideas, time and energy. No man is an island, and we all need a little help from our friends from time to time. The Internet has learnt the power of win-win. It works through the power of relationship and connections rather than the paradigm of good old fashioned competition. Win-win is attracting the attention of big business. News International paid $580 million (£340 million) for the online community website Myspace.com, a site where young people blog, swap music and connect to friends.[7] When action is taken from a place of wisdom then it is usually a win/win action. Win/win is the way to transform the world.

Take Powerful Actions

Pick one quality which you would like to awaken more of, such as courage, creativity, happiness, or peace. If you had this quality already, what things would you be doing differently in the world?

Choose three actions that would help you to stretch into this quality this week.

Do them and have fun. Then choose another three actions for the following week that help you stretch even more into this quality. Keep doing this until you wish to move on to another quality.

As you act from an inner quality, rather than from a desire to compete and win, you enter the realm of win-win. This is the place where your success and prosperity can encourage others to be successful and prosperous. Take an action where you win and others win also. Start small and aim big.

References

1. An English translation was published by Fourth Estate in 2002.
2. http://milliondollarhomepage.com
   http://news.bbc.co.uk/1/hi/magazine/4585026.stm
3. http://www.fastcompany.com/magazine/96/cirque-du-soleil.html
4. http://www.lesmis.com/pages/news/press_after16Triumphant.htm
5. http://hbswk.hbs.edu/item.jhtml?id=3780&t=bizhistory
6. http://www.orange.com/textonly/aboutorange/historyoforange.asp?bhcp=1
7. http://news.bbc.co.uk/2/hi/uk_news/magazine/4782118.stm

Part Three

Prosperity = The Way of

Life Force & Consciousness

Chapter 10

Prosperity = An Open Door

Man did not weave the web of life; he is merely a strand in it.
Whatever he does to the web, he does to himself.
ATTRIBUTED TO CHIEF SEATTLE

The Lion, the Witch and the Wardrobe, by C. S. Lewis, is an adventure story about four children who were evacuated from London during the blitz. The children - Peter, Susan, Edmund and Lucy - find themselves living with an elderly professor who lives in a big house with his housekeeper. Having little to occupy them, the children decide to explore the house and soon stumble upon a room with a large wardrobe. Whilst the other children move on, Lucy is curious and steps inside. To her amazement, through the wardrobe she sees another land, a land of trees and snow. She steps through the wardrobe and enters the mysterious land of Narnia, a place of trees, snow, deep magic and endless winter. When she returns to tell the others about her adventure, no one believes her. It is not long before circumstances conspire to draw the others into the wardrobe. Finally they see the magical land for themselves and in the blink of an eye their lives are changed forever.

Principle Ten   *Prosperity is an ancient way of living. It is about living in harmony with our environment and with different energy flows. It is the way of intuition.*

Prosperity = Returning from Exile

The scarcity mindset is based on the notion that the world operates in fixed and predictable ways. The prosperity mindset sees reality as being more fluid, where possibility is the name of the game. We have so far been exploring prosperity at a certain level. Now we are heading into prosperity hyper-drive. Here, possibility is as infinite as you can imagine. Beyond the open door lies a world that has always been there but which has been hidden for a long time. Our long gone ancestors knew of this world and worked with it. Yet this door has been closed for some years to people living in the modern world. There are two main reasons for this. First, mainstream religion had some strong things to say about any spiritual path that was not aligned with its own doctrines of faith. Second, the Age of Enlightenment had some strong views on anything it considered irrational or superstitious. Although this was a time of great advances in the sciences, it not only closed the door to the world of energy and spirit, it also locked the door. Indigenous peoples saw the earth to be their nurturing and bountiful Mother. The lagoons and caves were representations of the divine in all Her feminine forms. The fertile and wild were all considered to be aspects of Her body as were all the creatures that walked the earth. Indigenous peoples did not consider the earth to be a jungle where only the fittest survive. They saw the earth as a bountiful garden. They lived in intimate connection with nature, they came to love and respect Her and thank Her for all the gifts she bestowed upon them. To them the world was both a supportive place and a magical one where miracles could happen. When 'civilized' people first encountered indigenous peoples, they looked upon them as barbaric, foolish and ignorant and decided that the best thing to be done was either destroy them or convert them to the beliefs and ways of civilized people. When the Spaniards invaded Peru, the conquistador Pizarro handed the Inca King Atahualpa a Bible, saying that it contained the word of God. The King brought the book to his ear and listened. Hearing nothing, he threw the book down in disgust. This story illustrates how different these two worldviews were. Soon, the indigenous peoples were overwhelmed by the invading culture and were indoctrinated with a new story. One where humanity had been cast out of Paradise; people were punished for their sins; the universe was ruled by a distant Father God; and creation was polarized between eternally conflicting forces of good and evil. Under such a regime life became one of disconnection, hardship and repression.

Alberto Villoldo, a classically trained medical anthropologist studied shamanism amongst the descendants of the ancient Inca in Peru for twenty years. According to Alberto, the Native peoples understand themselves to be caretakers of the garden of the earth and those that managed to escape the missionaries never accepted the idea that they were thrown out of the garden.[1] Eric Julien, a French researcher who lived in Columbia with the Kogi (the descendants of the Maya), found a similar outlook. The Kogi have no concept of good and evil; they have a strong sense of harmony and balance and understand the consequences of being out of harmony. They view time as cyclical rather than linear and celebrate the vital cycles of birth, maturation, death and re-birth. They believe in honouring the different polarities of life, the masculine and the feminine and, like all shamanic people, see all living things as being infused with life force energy or spirit.[2]

To go to the next level of prosperity, we need to understand this ancient worldview, that everything is alive and responsive. This has enabled shamans to converse with nature, to speak with the spirits of the rivers, trees and mountains, and much more than speaking, *listen* to the energy patterns within nature. In Ancient China it was believed that the universe was an energy field called *Tao*, a word which translates into English as 'The Way', 'The Way of Nature', 'The Universe' or 'The Path of Natural Reality'. Taoism was founded in China around 600BC although it drew on ideas that had been in existence for thousands of years. The Tao was sometimes called 'The Watercourse Way' because it described energy as flowing like water, since water always seeks the path of least resistance. The Tao describes life as a dance between two energies, yin and yang. Yin is feminine, receptive, introverted, imaginative, and receiving: yang is masculine, dynamic, extraverted, focused, and purposeful.

The Hermetic philosophy of Ancient Egypt held a similar view. Thrice Great Hermes, the alchemist and magician, said that the whole of creation exists in a state of vibration, a dance of attraction between the masculine and feminine polarities. Here creation is a dynamic interplay of forces where nothing exists in a state of rest. In ancient China, this energy is called *chi*, in Hawaii it is called *Mana*, in ancient India it is called *Prana* and in Japan it is known as *Ki*. This energy was tracked as it flowed through the body and the earth itself. The early inhabitants of Britain determined the placement of sacred sites such as Avebury and Stonehenge according to energy flows within the earth.

Science and spirituality have increasingly become partners in the exploration of the unseen. Since Einstein's famous equation, $E=MC^2$, it is recognized that all matter contains energy. For instance, it is estimated that within the body of an average sized adult there is the equivalent potential energy, if anyone could work out a way to release it, of around thirty large hydrogen bombs. Even a uranium bomb, probably the deadliest weapon yet devised, only releases around 1% of its potential energy in an explosion. More and more, quantum physicists are describing matter in terms of fluid energy and dancing light.

James Lovelock introduced the Gaia Hypothesis, which sees the earth as a self-regulating, biological organism rather than an inanimate entity as traditional earth science holds. Similarly, chaos theory points to a very different image of the universe. It is perhaps best known for its *butterfly effect,* which proposes that something as seemingly insignificant as the flap of a butterfly's wings on one side of the globe could create a tornado on the other. Researchers have been increasingly looking at light and vibration. Dr. Masaru Emoto, a Japanese researcher, has explored how water is affected by different types of vibrations.[3] He studied various things, such as monks reciting prayers over bowls of water. He also had photographs of different people and locations placed under containers of water. After the water was subjected to a certain vibration it was then frozen and the resulting crystallized water photographed. The results were astounding. The photographs showed that the water reacted in a very distinct way to the vibrations it was being subjected to. Some water crystals were beautifully formed. Others seemed chaotic and fragmented. His research is very important, particularly when you consider that water constitutes around 70% of both the human body and of the earth. Similarly, physicist Dr. Barbara Brennan has devoted 30 years to researching the human energy field. She has written two best-selling books, *Hands of Light,* and *Light Emerging* (both by Bantam, 1993). She now runs a highly successful international school teaching energy healing skills.

Sandra Ingerman is a marine biologist who has looked into reversing river pollution using shamanic techniques. In her book, *Medicine for the Earth: How to Transform Personal and Environmental Toxins* (Random House, 2001), she outlines her experiments that show how consciousness can reverse the toxicity of intentionally polluted water. Lynne McTaggart interviewed fifty pioneering scientists before writing her book, *The Field* (HarperCollins, 2001). The Field is a term for the ocean of subatomic vibrations that exists in the space between things. Here, human beings cease to be so distinct and separate from their environment, and become instead points of pulsating and interacting energy – a bit like the concept of The Force in the film Star Wars. Many scientists are coming to the conclusion that the universe is stranger than we are able to imagine.

Governments have recently become interested in the realm of energy and consciousness. In 1969, U.S. intelligence sources concluded that the Russian government was investing large amounts of time and money into developing psychic spies. In response, the U.S. government began its own research into using psychic abilities for defence purposes. The U.S.

Department of Defense defined this as 'the learned ability to transcend space and time, to view persons, places or things remote in space-time; to gather and report information on the same', in other words, to spy and gather information.[4]

The corporate world is not far behind. According to Gay Hendricks and Kate Ludeman, authors of *The Corporate Mystic* (Bantam, 1997), we are just as likely to find a mystic in a corporate boardroom as in a monastery. After studying many top successful business people for over 25 years, they discovered that many are highly intuitive and follow non-dogmatic forms of spirituality in which deeds are more important than words.

Prosperity = The Way of the Seer

Sensing energy is a skill of prosperity. The shamanic skills of knowing, reading and sensing this energy field are as relevant now as they were when Stone Age hunters stalked mammoths for food. We may not have to work within a cold Siberian landscape and we might not be particularly interested in finding a herd of animals to hunt, but we might be interested in knowing where to look for a new apartment or for a new job. The context may have changed but the essence has not. Humans have been sensing their environments for thousands of years. We have just forgotten this innate ability. All living things are able to sense the energies of their environment; if they did not, they would not be able to survive. In the animal, bird, fish and insect kingdoms, sensing energy is called instinct. Take a small garden spider weaving a web in the great outdoors. It has the amazing ability to weave a beautiful, symmetrical web in the most unpredictable of environments. It can weave a web in a micro-terrain that would baffle many a modern day engineer. This little creature has to compute distances between anchorage points, and to take into account factors like wind and rain, and sometimes it needs to work in the dark. This is even more amazing when you consider that these tiny creatures have poor eyesight. Despite this they manage to create such amazing webs. They can sense vibrations travelling through air, substrate surfaces and even water. They can tell the difference between the wing beats of an approaching moth or of a wasp predator. They know when their web has been touched by rain, wind or by an insect.

Human beings are deeply intuitive by nature. We have unlearned this skill through our conditioning, education and cultural values but it is there none the less. Intuition is the art of sensing energy in ourselves and in the environment. Sensing energy is an essential skill in the modern world. This is because we are required to handle more information on a daily basis and make decisions faster. We do not have to worry nowadays about becoming lunch for some large predator but there are other dangers that we face on a daily basis. Living in a big city can be deadly if we do not have our wits about us. We may not be able to track a person or an animal as skillfully as an Australian Aborigine but we can learn to navigate our way through problems and even danger. We can learn to smell danger, feel the certainty of success, or see the way through and proceed. If we know how to use our intuition well we will know the next step to take before the intellect has had time to work it all out. We can avoid getting too involved with individuals who do not have the right 'feel' and be at complete ease with a total stranger because the 'vibe' is right.

Have you ever entered a crowded room and felt suddenly uplifted or deflated? Have you ever visited a place and suddenly felt touched without knowing why? Have you ever thought of something only to hear someone else voice the same thing? Perhaps you have silently sung a song to yourself and then someone suddenly begins to sing it. Have you ever thought of someone and soon after had them call on the telephone? Have you ever felt 'something is not right' and, forewarned, avoided a problem? Have you ever lost something and then just knew where it was and found it? All these are instances of sensing energy. Intuition at its most basic can be a 'yes' or 'no' response. It can also be as simple as, 'when I think about this thing I get a bad or heavy feeling' or, 'when I think about taking this choice I get an overwhelming sense of peace and calm.' Western society has trained many of us to ignore our natural intuitive abilities by focusing exclusively on the intellect with its functions of logic, planning and reason. Intuition is a synthesis of right and left brain abilities. The left brain gives us the ability to focus, plan, decide, dare, analyze, recognize, structure, understand and design. The right brain gives us the ability to imagine, dream, and know, feel and intuit. Most people are lopsided in that they rely on one side more than the other. Intuition is a state of receiving impulses from the dreamy and imaginative right brain. To be effective our intuition has to be connected to our left brain linear thinking and action orientated side.

One way in which shamans learn to awaken their intuition is to work on sharpening their outer senses. Intuition is linked to the senses and so if we can see, hear, feel, smell and taste the world more clearly then our intuition becomes clearer. The idea is that if the outer senses were awake then the inner senses would open also. In the modern world, we dull our senses through poor use and over stimulation. How often do you see people walking down the road unaware of their reality because they are pre-occupied with talking on a mobile phone or blocking out external sounds by listening to music? These activities would make no sense to indigenous peoples whose ability to stay present and awake often makes the difference between life and death. Indigenous peoples have an ability to read external reality that seems magical by our standards.

Activating Your Intuition

Intuition only works when we are in a still, peaceful and neutral space. A busy mind, churning emotions and a tense body all hinder our intuition. Practising relaxation is an important beginning stage to sensing energy. Practise noticing the difference between being in a still and neutral space and being in a reactive, fearful or desiring state. Intuition only works well in the neutral space.

Sit in silence as a daily practice. In silence, listen to your breath, hold a restful word in mind (such as serenity or peace) to come to a neutral space. Find ways to relax the mind.

Start to get to know your inner world of thoughts, sounds, images, and feelings. The more you get to know your inner world, the easier it will be to notice subtle shifts and communications.

Sit in silence at home and also in nature. Feel the difference. Sit in silence in different settings. Sit in silence with trees and lakes and other kinds of landscapes. Sit in silence in the busy towns and cities and feel the difference. Notice how you respond differently on the inside to different environments.

Practise being inward looking: that no matter what is going on externally, you stay connected to your internal world. Practise staying connected to your inner world of thoughts and feelings as you go through the day. Notice what kind of thoughts, feelings and sensations are going on and what external triggers influence them.

In the early stages, be careful with whom you share your intuitive insights. If they are shared too soon, we can leave ourselves open to criticism and self-doubt.

Intuition opens, grows and deepens with time and practise. Essential qualities to develop intuition are curiosity, exploration, trust and patience.

Awakening the Inner Senses

The inner senses can be awakened through imaginative exercises. For instance, imagine crossing a desert, or walking along a sea shore, or climbing a mountain, or moving across a glacier.

Explore the landscape through each of the senses. How clearly do you see, hear, feel, taste and smell the landscape? Try different landscapes.

Notice things like the temperature, the humidity, the song of birds, the sound of silence, and the feel of the wind and the smell of sea or earth. Practise noticing different colours, sounds, and textures.

Using Your Primary Door

It is important to know which of your senses is the strongest. Think of something you are going to do later today. Do you think about this thing in terms of inner pictures, sounds, feelings, smells, or taste?

A clue to your primary sense is found in the language you habitually use. What do you say to someone to communicate that you understand? 'I see what you mean', 'I hear what you are saying' or 'I have a feel for what you mean'?

If your primary sense is visual, work on opening your imagination. Pick something into which you would like a deeper insight. Think about the subject and close your eyes. Allow your imagination to paint pictures, present memories or imagery. Just play for a while. After a while, the imagery may change. Notice what your imagination says about this area. You can do the same for listening to the conversations that you have about a certain area, or noticing the feelings in the body.

Intuition at its most basic is a yes/no response. Find something that you know is an obvious 'yes' for you – such as, 'Do I like eating strawberries?'. (Avoid anything too big and emotive, such as, 'Will I be rich?') When you think about eating strawberries, how does that feeling of 'yes-ness' translate into an image or feeling? Then pick something that is an obvious 'no', such as doing a boring activity. How does this translate as a feeling of 'no-ness' in the body or imagination? If you wish to go deeper, repeat this exercise using more subtle distinctions such as light versus heavy or expansive versus limited, or 'feels scary but good' versus 'feels safe but limiting'.

It is also important to spend some time developing the other intuitive senses. The primary sense never works alone: it is just the main door.

Synergize your intuition, pick something you wish to work on and sit in silent contemplation. What does your imagination and mind have to say about this subject? What emotional and physical feelings do you sense? Put all of these things together, and you are listening to your intuition speaking to you.

Prosperity is interested in the interconnection of things. There is essentially no separation between our environment and the web of life force energy. Being alert to our environment is an important skill to learn. It does not matter whether we are moving through a wood or a corporate boardroom, a rocky valley or a busy city street. Danger can live in any landscape. The ecologist, philosopher, and accomplished sleight of hand magician, David Abram, lived with indigenous shamans in Indonesia, Nepal and the Americas. He so impressed the local shamans with his trickery that they invited him into their homes and into their magical worldview. He learnt the ancient ways of sensing energy. In his book *The Spell of the Sensuous* (Vintage, 1997), he describes how a native hunter would react to hearing a strange noise while walking in the forest. The hunter would stop, not knowing whether the sound came from friend or foe, predator or harmless animal. He would quieten his breathing, and listen for the sound when it came again. He would drop into a state of silent observation without wasting energy on thinking or imagining what the noise might be about. He would scan the branches around and the leafy canopy overhead with a soft unfocused gaze, waiting to catch something out of place, a slight rustle of greenery, or some other movement against the backdrop of the forest. All of his senses would be alive and working in synergy and in relationship with the environment.

We live in a world where energy pervades everything; it vibrates through people, families, corporations and governments. It ripples through buildings along streets and through such intangibles as the Internet. If you pay attention, you will notice that towns and cities have different energy broadcasts. You will notice that different parts of a city will have a different feel from others. Walking through a large concrete housing estate will probably feel quite different from walking along a street of terraced houses with leafy gardens. Walk through any town or city and take a moment to feel the energy that is either flowing through or stagnating in the neighbourhood. Some streets and areas will feel vibrant and uplifting and others dull and depressing. Some places will have a more prosperous and enlivening feel while others will feel as if the energy is spiralling down. If you look closely, you will notice that some places will have a clearer look than others.

We sense energy in different ways. Some people are good at sensing energy through the way they physically feel in a place or with people. Some are better at sensing energy through doing an activity. Energy can be light or heavy, bright or dark, smooth or grating, flowing or resistant, draining or energizing. Some people notice energy through how they begin to breathe differently. Shallow breathing and deep breathing are signs of entering different energy flows. Some people are good at sensing energy through their imagination and see all kinds of images. Some things will seem bright or dark, clear or misty, sparkly or dull when seen through the mind's eye. Some people can sense energy as if they were watching an inner movie. Some people see colours around people, and can see the energy fields around living things. Some read energy through the quality of their thinking. When their thinking is muddled and confused, so is the energy around them. When their thinking is clear and crisp so is the energy around them. Some sense energy through their internal feelings and are good at noticing subtle shifts and changes. The intuition may act through a sense of restlessness, or physical discomfort. It may feel like 'goose bumps', or have a strong emotional feel. The important thing is to know how you sense energy. One of the main ways I sense energy is through my feelings. Just before the news broke about the tragic events of 9/11 I remember walking down the high street in a state of shock without knowing why.

Different Ways of Sensing Vibration

The three main ways of sensing energy are:

Clairvoyance: clear seeing through the imagination of either metaphorical or literal imagery, in which a person sees events and things beyond their physical view.

Clairaudience: clear hearing of thoughts or information about a person or situation; it can be experienced as delicate sounds or other attention-getting sound. It can come as a voice that is literally heard, either directly or in the mind. This voice may sound like the person's own, or like someone else's.

Clairsentience: clear sensing is probably the most familiar way in which intuition operates, through hunches, gut feelings, or just a sense of knowing. It may be accompanied by a physical sensation, such as a tingling of the skin.

There are a number of ways to use energy sensing abilities, for example:

Precognition is the ability to know about an event before it actually occurs. This is not the same as predictions based on deductive reasoning or current knowledge. It can happen whilst being in a conscious state as well as in the dream state. Precognition can be especially useful when it comes as a clear warning or as a green light to move forward in a particular venture.

Psychometry is the ability to discern information from the energetic vibration of an object. Objects hold information in the form of energy that can be read. This can be useful when wishing to gain information about a person, a company, or a product, for example.

Telepathy is where we learn to read the vibrations from the energy field of another; this ability transcends time and space. Telepathy enables a person to pick up on the misgivings or doubts of another; it might also explain how great ideas in science and business are thought up at the same time at different places.

Prosperity = Effective Intuition

Intuition is about getting results. It is not about getting fascinated by psychic material. A result can be saving a life; avoiding a problem; achieving a desired goal, or helping someone else get what they want. Amazingly, some people develop their intuition to a high degree and then use it effectively to block where they want to go. One experienced psychic rose through the ranks of an organization and used her intuition to scan the environment for potential threats and problems. Soon, her intuition was busy gathering pieces of information that reinforced her ongoing feeling of concern. Not only did she feel an increasing sense of unease, but within a few years, the organization in which she worked became saturated with a mild form of paranoia and stress. This is not the way to use our intuition effectively. This is using it to create more stress and problems. Intuition is meant to make our lives easier, not harder. One person had a well developed intuition which was remarkably accurate. However, she often used it to check out if people were being honest with her. Her baseline assumption was that people were not usually honest with her. Using her intuition as a form of radar, she often picked up subtle hints that that confirmed her view of people. She lost many friends because she assumed that people were being dishonest and treated them accordingly. She did not consider that sometimes people just have a bad day. A good friend pointed this out to her. She was shocked to realize that she had been using her intuition in this way. When she changed the way she used her intuition she found she could just as easily sense when people were being open and authentic with her. This helped her to trust these people even more. Now when she senses something is not right she is inclined to give that person some space. In order to be effective in life, we must engage our intuition properly towards the things we want to achieve, taking into account both the short and long term view. We must never use it primarily as a protection filter against the world or other people.

Philip cycles to work every day. He uses his intuition to help him get to where he wants to go. He is acutely aware that there are dangers on the busy streets of Central London. There are moving vehicles that can knock him over and stationary vehicles that are equally dangerous – a driver opening a door suddenly can mean serious injury or even death to the cyclist. Philip's intuition tells him when to be cautious and when to fly like an eagle.

Intuition can be used to warn us of danger. Intuition can make the difference between life and death. A fire crew was called to a fire at the back of a house. The chief officer led his hose team into the building. Standing in the living room, they blasted water onto the smoke and flames but the fire roared back and continued to burn. They were baffled by the fire's persistence and went on fighting the flames. Suddenly the chief officer was gripped by an uneasy feeling. His intuition told him to get out of the house immediately. He ordered everyone to leave and just as the crew reached the street, the living-room floor caved in. Had they stayed inside, the men would have plunged into a blazing basement.

James went walking in the foothills of the Italian Alps one Christmas Eve with his ten year old stepson, Paul, who was a novice yet enthusiastic climber. They walked for about an hour until the valley below seemed far away. James was following Paul's natural exuberance for climbing. They climbed up a steep incline beside a small waterfall and came to a narrow ledge. Standing there, James felt a growing sense of unease. As he looked around he saw that the sun was just about setting over the distant peaks. He estimated that they had about an hour and a half of daylight left. He looked down, uncertain as to how they were going to get back. The rocks below were wet and he did not have the right footwear for such a climb. At that moment the climb down looked almost impossible. He felt a growing sense of panic and so sat for some minutes breathing deeply until the strong emotion passed. He asked his intuition to show him how to get his stepson down safely. He then saw that it was possible to swing Paul down on to a lower ledge using his coat as a makeshift rope. The young boy was then able to scramble down fairly easily but James remained stuck. Paul ran for help but James knew that it would be almost dark before anyone arrived. He stilled his mind and asked for the solution. After a few moments, he opened his eyes and began to see a way down. It was as if the path down was illuminated by a soft light. It was an unorthodox route to take but he trusted his sense of rightness and set off. The first few steps were difficult and then the climb grew easier. Soon he was down and he met the rescue party on the way up.

Sensing energy is a skill. As we work with sensing energy, we will come to know the difference between vibrations that feel good and uplifting and those that feel uncomfortable or even painful. This can be useful because it means we have extra information at our disposal. Our intuition can warn us when we are stepping into situations that will only bring misery and it can also point the way to greater success and reward. It can even save us money. Susan was about to become involved in a business project with some other people. On the surface, things looked reasonably optimistic yet she had a growing gut feeling that something was not right. She decided to trust this feeling and asked her intuition whether she should proceed with the venture. She sat with the project in meditation and felt her unease grow. She decided to do a little investigating and she found that things were not as they seemed; some of the people were in serious financial difficulties. Susan was able to review her position once she knew the true financial picture and quickly withdrew from the project.

Robert had been unhappy with his office for some while. He just did not like the feel of the place. Not only was the feel not right, the office was also in a very expensive part of town so the rent was high. One day, some friends who were sensitive to energy visited and said that the building felt like an old hospital. He asked a work colleague to check it out and discovered that it had indeed been a hospital many years before. This motivated Robert to look for a new office. He looked at all the conventional routes but was not finding what he wanted. One day on the way to work, he felt like taking a different route. He passed a building that caught his eye and he noticed an 'office to let' sign. He went in but found that the last office space had only just been let. He asked if they managed any other office blocks nearby. They did, and Robert went on to find an office space three times as big, in a building that had a much better feel and where the rent was 40% lower.

Developing an Effective Intuition

Developing a strong intuition and linking it to a strong sense of direction, intention and purpose gives a useful frame in which to work. Intuition is an unconscious ability that needs conscious direction.

Choose some important goals. Sit in meditation and ask that your intuition begins to show the way to achieving these goals. Start to listen and notice any inner messages from your intuition, trying to prompt you in the direction of or away from certain things. Listen to your dreams, your gut feelings, your sense of 'rightness' or 'yes-ness'.

Ask that your intuition protects you from unnecessary problems or danger. Begin to notice how your intuition communicates unease or a warning. Make sure you know the internal signs that tell you to slow down or avoid a particular situation – such as discomfort in the solar plexus, a sense of dullness or heaviness, or a feeling of light panic.

Your intuition will not work quite like anyone else's and you need to get to know yourself a little better. Begin to act on your intuition. Learn by trial and error.

Intuition and Choice

Pick an area where you need to make a decision. What are your options?

Sit and contemplate each one. For a choice between two possibilities, imagine holding one choice in one hand. Note the sensations you have, the feelings of lightness or dullness, and any images or sounds. Then do the same for the second choice, holding it in the other hand.

If there is a third option, simply imagine shaking out the energy of the other two possibilities and repeating the exercise for this third possibility.

Notice which choice feels the lighter or the brighter or more the expansive.

References

1. Villoldo, Alberto. Shaman, Healer, Sage. Bantam, 2001
2. http://www.cyberclass.net/kogicanada.htm
3. Emoto, Dr Masaru. The Hidden Messages in Water. Beyond Words Publishing, 2004
4. http://www.mceagle.com/remote-viewing/stargate/stargate-qa.shtml

Chapter 11

Prosperity = Solid Grace

Many heroes are not yet born.
Many have already died.
To be alive to hear this song is a victory.

TRADITIONAL WEST AFRICAN SONG

Before the outbreak of the Second World War, a famous German researcher went to Japan. The scientist was a great admirer of Japanese swords and knew of their superiority to European swords. He took several back to Germany and handed them to an establishment working in the research and development of high technology steel. The materials and method of production were analyzed. With this scientific data, the German scientist was sure that he could reproduce a sword of the same quality. The outcome was a dismal failure. The scientist had failed to take into account the mystical nature of forging a sword. Making a sword is a sacred act that enables *kami*, or a higher power, to enter into the sword. This imbued each sword with a spirit of its own. Before working, the sword-smiths would undergo fasting and ritual purification. They would then work in white clothes in front of a Shinto shrine. Soldiers defeated in battle would pray at shrines, asking why their swords had lost their spirit.

Principle Eleven   *Prosperity is generated through our personal presence and power in the world. This personal power is enhanced and refreshed by our connection to cosmic power. This is the way of the spiritual warrior.*

Prosperity = The Warrior's Way

Solid grace is a call to personal power. This is the way of the spiritual warrior. Warriors defend communities and help to create prosperity in the world in which they live. Many ancient societies honoured the warrior tradition. In such societies, warriors did not tend to commit mass slaughter on the battlefield in the manner of modern armies: they were the protectors of society and they worked with power – not the kind that bullies or manipulates but the kind that serves the life force. Power is a dirty word in today's world but prosperity is not created out of wishful thinking; it comes from working with one's own power and the power that exists in the world around us. A warrior is both a defender of the old and a creator of the new. The warrior is naturally courageous and daring.

Mongol warriors carried a Spirit Banner, constructed by tying strands of hair from the best stallions to the shaft of a spear, just below its blade. The Spirit Banner always remained in the open air beneath the sky that the Mongols worshiped. As the strands of hair blew and tossed in the constant breeze of the steppe, they captured the power of the wind, the sky and the sun; it was this power that inspired the warrior's dreams and beckoned him ever onwards.

The warrior Maori culture of New Zealand believes that everything has an active life force and a living spirit. The word *Mana* roughly translates as 'personal spiritual power' or 'prestige'. Nature and individuals possess *Mana*. The Gods have *Mana*. Tribal chiefs possess *Mana* which flows through them to their tribe. *Mana* can be inherited and acquired by an individual. A person can acquire *Mana* through displaying courage and prowess in war, and through being industrious and creative in peace. A person can lose *Mana* by misusing their talents and skills, and through insults, injuries or carelessness.

American Plains Indian warriors saw combat as being of great spiritual significance because it meant protecting tribal land or tribal members. Some Indian Plains tribes taught that bravery, cunning, and stealth were more important than killing an enemy. In some tribes, the best coup came from simply touching an enemy in the heat of battle. Most tribes believed in a clear distinction between the activities of war and those of peace. Consequently, ceremonies were devised to aid individuals and entire communities in making the transition from peace to war and back again. Warriors were ritually prepared for war and offered protective medicine to assure their safe return to the community. Many tribes also used purification ceremonies to restore individual warriors, as well as the rest of the community, to a peaceful state. It was believed that, unless the returning warriors were purged of the trauma of battle, they would not be able to assimilate back into peaceful patterns of behaviour within the community.

We live in a very different world. We live in a world that constantly talks about peace yet has so much aggression and violence within its homes, communities and workplaces. In the scarcity game, pseudo warriors are taught to fight but have no means of switching off their violence afterwards. There are no peace rituals for today's warriors. Pseudo warriors seek release through aggression. Some do it through drinking and fighting in bar brawls. Others look out over the corporate world and seek to 'make a killing', 'destroy the competition', 'take over a company' or make a 'cyber attack'. Pseudo warriors are to be found wherever making money is an issue. Making and working for money in the scarcity game evokes a destructive warrior spirit which can feel like swimming in a pool with sharks. The pseudo warrior can be found in the bad tempered boss, the hotshot junior executive, the company 'yes' man or woman, or the sexual predator. Pseudo warriors hate anything that seems weak or vulnerable, preferring instead the hard image. Yet this tough exterior is a shield for a very wounded and vulnerable interior. Many pseudo warriors operate like a Little Lord Fauntleroy who screams for his mother to feed him, kiss him and attend to his every need. Pseudo warriors seek to defeat others through the superiority of their intellect. They are masters of the razor sharp wit that can cut a person down at ten paces. Some have neither sufficient wit nor intellect and so seek safety in numbers and hunt their victims in packs. Pseudo warriors are just as likely be found in a prison riot as on a trade union picket line.

The world needs true warriors in every field of endeavour. Without them, the world is likely to continue the way it is going. The true warrior knows the art of true discipline and, unlike pseudo warriors, has learnt to put his or her personal feelings aside in order to serve the greater good. There is an old story of a samurai whose master was murdered by an assassin. The samurai tracked the assassin down and, as he raised his sword to deal the death blow, the assassin spat in the samurai's face. The samurai sheathed his sword and turned and walked away. As soon as the samurai felt his own personal anger rise, he was no longer dispassionate and so could not strike the assassin.

To be a warrior in a society that does not honour a warrior tradition takes courage and perseverance. Because we have mostly been brought up to understand power as something external, we have a distorted understanding of it. Ancient cultures knew that there was a field of living energy that underpinned physical existence. This field exists in a dynamic state of constant vibration and movement. The Sora, who live in eastern India, see power as moving like electricity. It is able to flow along certain channels, and leap gaps. This power can also be stored if you know how. The Salish people of the Pacific Northwest see power as living in harmony with nature in order to create magic and beauty everywhere. The Dakota people in North America see power as 'points of concentration in the movement of spirit.' The Mongols had the word *tegsh*, which meant living in balance with life force. The word *Maori* means 'natural' and the Maori people of New Zealand have a blessing '*Tihei Maori Ora*' which translates as 'celebrate life force'. Working with this kind of power leads to the creation of very exciting and tangible results.

Martial artists have worked with life force energy for as long as five thousand years. *Chi Kung* translates as 'excellence of energy', or the skill of governing one's life force. Taoist internal martial arts, like T'ai Chi, teach practitioners how to harness chi in order to follow the way of the Tao.

The Three Internal Treasures

In Taoist philosophy, there are three vital centres or 'treasures' in the body which are the places where we are most open to receiving energy:

The Crown: Keeps the warrior connected to the inspiration and guidance of heaven. It is useful to imagine the head as being suspended by a thread reaching up into the heavens. With each in-breath, imagine breathing energy down through this thread into your body.

The Belly: Called the *Tan Tien*, this seat of power is traditionally said to lie one and a half inches below the navel and one and a half inches in from the front of the body, towards the spine. This is the body's balancing point. It is the centre of power where energy can be stored. It is also a place of stillness and great depth. Practise moving with awareness from this place.

The Feet: Located in the centre of the soles of the feet, these centres allow 'earth chi' to rise up into the body. This keeps the warrior rooted on the earth. In Tai Chi, energy is accessed not through force or effort but through relaxation and right balance. Practise just standing on the ground. Take off your shoes and stand barefoot for some minutes each day on the earth. Relax your feet. Imagine energy rising up into your body on each in-breath.

The Way of Heaven and Earth

Move through your day with awareness of these energy centres. Try breathing energy down through the crown or up through the feet into the T'an Tien. Working with these centres increases our sense of presence and of being in the eternal present moment. From these centres, the presence of the Tao can be felt moving through existence.

Imagine that you are a tree with roots going deep into the earth. With each step that you take, imagine that your energy becomes anchored into the earth and that you are immovable. Become grounded into the energy field of the earth.

Imagine that you have branches rising from your crown to the centre of the cosmos. Imagine that the energy of creation is flowing down into you. You are connected to the centre of all existence. Nothing can move you. Become infused with the energy field of the cosmos.

The Radiant Sun Exercise

Meditate and witness the chatter of the mind and the moving currents of emotional force. Find the stillness in the centre of this activity by just sitting, breathing and witnessing.

Take long and slow conscious breaths into the belly and breathe out fully and consciously. Allow your breath to release any tension in the belly. Your centre is charged through conscious breathing.

Meditate at sunrise and connect with the chi that flows from the sun. Imagine that you can breathe this energy into your belly like a stream of golden light that flows to you with every in-breath. Imagine that you can store this energy in the belly and that it begins to pulsate like a radiant sun.

Imagine breathing out any old energy to the sun. Release the old to make way for the new.

Laugh to develop a strong centre; Taoist masters talk about developing an 'inner smile'. Go about your day and see the humour in life. Laugh for no reason and feel the effect that smiling has on strengthening the belly.

Sing whenever you can to energize your centre. Sing songs that uplift and empower. Sing some old favourites. Make up some new lyrics to your favourite songs.

Working with these centres of force can produce astonishing results. For instance, before he found fame, the well known martial artist Bruce Lee used to tour around giving demonstrations to promote his school. Despite being of slim stature, he developed his ability to use chi to demonstrate his famous 'one-inch punch', where he could punch someone from only one inch away yet still have enough force to send them back several feet.

In the West, we are taught to think of strength and power as being in our arms and shoulders, and in our brains. Yet, according to ancient Chinese texts, the secret of good health, happiness and success lies in having a strong centre. A Japanese Sumo wrestler's strength lies in the belly. In Japanese culture, *Hara no aru hito* literally means 'a man with centre', or 'a man with belly'.

In the West, we are taught to centre ourselves either in the head or in the genitals. Focusing on the intellect and academic pursuits keeps us centred in the head. Being bombarded with sexual imagery through advertising and the media draws our attention down to the genital area. Being pulled to either means that we do not live from our true centre. When people lose touch with the centre, they often feel anxious and alienated from their body and feelings. Stress and busyness knock us off centre, too. Prosperity is about living from the centre. Zen teaches the art of being empty and centred in the belly. A famous Zen master was asked how he maintained a high level of awareness. He answered, 'When eating I eat, when fetching water I fetch water, and when I go to bed I sleep'. Living from the centre means living with presence. The centre anchors us in the here and now, and connects us with the cosmic life force. The warrior inhabits a strong inner centre. Being seated in the belly means that we can feel our inner power and direct it at will. A person who has learnt how to live from his or her centre can speak with presence and authority, gain the confidence of other people or even win a karate tournament. This is the power of pure focused energy, which can also be called charisma or self-confidence.

Tara used to be afraid of speaking in front of large groups and worried about making a mistake and not being perfect. Then she began to discipline herself in the art of centring herself. She began to attend talks and notice how the best public speakers performed their art. She then made the bold step of confronting a lifelong fear, that of speaking at Speakers' Corner in Hyde Park. When she arrived there were many other speakers standing on their 'soap boxes' and talking on a range of subjects. She took a deep breath, stood on her 'soap box' and began to speak. Her chosen subject was the 'nature of truth' because so many other speakers there were telling others about 'the truth'. Soon, a large crowd gathered around her and she spent the first 15 minutes easing herself into the situation. She soon relaxed into it and began to really enjoy the challenge. She even found she enjoyed being heckled. After 45 minutes, she simply stopped and was told by several people who had heard her speak how engaging they thought she was.

A person with a strong centre learns that power flows where attention goes. Simple attention can change a situation. A person with a focused attention will help to focus a group. A person with a peaceful attention will help to bring calm to a group. Successful people have learnt to use their attention to create results. They take their attention away from situations or people that drain them.

Using intention is an ancient skill which links the directing power of the head with the dynamo of the belly. In many aboriginal rock art paintings, hunters are often portrayed with weapons and erect penises that point towards the hunted animal. This recurring theme is not about unnatural sexual urges of Stone Age men but is an ancient practice of connecting the intention to hunt with the dynamic power of the belly to achieve the desired outcome. Fantasy, on the other hand, is about engaging the head without the belly. Power comes from the synergy of the two. Having a strong centre and a strong intention is like flicking on a switch and directing electricity down a certain circuit: it cannot help but illuminate the light bulb. Intention is about energy flow and possibility rather than control. It is not about attachment to outcomes. To have the intention of getting a job that is creative and well rewarded is one thing: to insist that a certain person or company must give it to you is another. With intention there is no need for hard work. Intention makes the impossible possible. Intention helps us generate miracles in the world. I have heard so many true stories about the power of intention. Several years ago a man living in the north of England wanted to attend a training course in the south of England. Although the course was expensive, around £1500, this did not deter him from wanting to attend. Even though he was on unemployment benefit he used what little money he had to buy a train ticket to London. Once there he went to a church to pray. He sat down and after a little while another man sat down beside him and they entered into conversation. He told his story and when he had finished speaking the other guy wrote out a cheque and handed it to him. The cheque was for the full amount of the course.

Intention and Attention

You can choose what you wish to focus your attention upon.
What do you choose to notice in the world?
Set your intention to notice more joy or happiness or love.
The stronger your intention, the more your attention will be drawn to these qualities in the world.
The more you notice these qualities, the more you become them.
Attention informs our thinking, believing and acting.

'Chunking Down' Your Intent

Intention is similar to outcome-oriented thinking but it is done with an awareness of energy and centre. With intention, mental, emotional and psychic energy begins to flow towards what you want.

From the bigger picture of your life, begin to 'chunk down' your intentions into the week ahead. What intentions do you have for the week? What intentions do you have for the day ahead?

Do you want more peace, more friendship, more energy, more adventure, or more joy? You can always set the intention of surprise and surrender!

What intentions do you have for breakfast, for the morning, for lunch, for the afternoon, for the evening? What are your intentions for a specific meeting or telephone call?

What intentions do you hold around different areas of your life, such as leisure, money, relationships, or studying?

Adam trained in karate for some years and learnt a lot about physical techniques but very little about energy and internal power. He then gave up karate and spent twelve years learning about energy and meditation. He then returned to karate training for nine months, and then entered a regional karate championship. Before the tournament, he spent time in meditation and breathing to increase his sensitivity and inner vitality.

During the tournament, he felt could feel his centre as a radiant sun. He felt anchored on the earth and connected to the cosmos. To the amazement of his friends, he won two gold medals. Adam not only learned how to develop a strong centre and focused intent; he had gone further and linked that with his intuition. He could feel his opponent before he moved. This success in the karate ring deepened his trust in his energy practice. He felt this same power at work in other areas of his life. He began to access it in his career. He felt more confident in taking on extra responsibilities. Because he radiated a silent power people tended to look upon him as a natural leader.

The entrepreneur who is unattached to results yet who is moved by a big vision is a warrior. A friend of mine told me about a free, two-day money seminar she attended. The event was set up and run by two people, one the seminar presenter and the other an experienced marketing person. Both were warriors in the sense that they were willing to take a risk and not be attached to results. The seminar cost around £30,000 to hold; because it was free, there was the potential for making a huge loss. The hope was that enough people would come and be so thrilled by the event that they would buy other trainings and products. In the end, the seminar attracted 1,500 people and they sold over £200,000 worth of places on training courses and also on products.

Intuition and Power

When you get a strong intuition about something, begin to engage your power of action behind it. Step with awareness and stay connected to your intuition.

Allow your intuition to inform your movement. Does it tell you to go slowly and patiently or with full speed and power? Be informed by feedback and results.

Practise synergizing your intuition and power. Like driving a sports car with a powerful engine, go slowly at first. Learn how to handle this new skill through practise.

Prosperity = Gifts of the Shadow

A tribal elder sat and began to share a story with some of the younger warriors of his tribe. As they began to gather and to sit around him to hear his wisdom, he began.

'A battle is raging inside of me, a great battle between two bear warrior spirits. The first bear warrior spirit expresses his warrior journey with anger, arrogance, envy, fear, false-pride, guilt, lies, and resentment. The other bear warrior spirit expresses his warrior journey with benevolence, faith, friendship, hope, joy, humility, love, and peace. This battle exists in every warrior, young and old alike.'

The young men thought about this for a minute, and then one young warrior asked, 'Which bear warrior spirit will win?'

Another young and eager warrior cried out, 'I know, it's the one you feed?'

The old warrior paused before answering.

'You are part right; feeding one will make it stronger, but you must learn to understand both bear warrior spirits, finding a balance in life, and your warrior journey. If you ignore and starve the first bear warrior spirit and do not tame it, it can creep up and consume you. If you ignore and starve the second bear spirit and do not nurture its qualities, you can become a lonely, bitter and shallow shell.'

Warriors learn to face the ultimate adversary: themselves. This is what it means to face the shadow self. The shadow is everything that we pretend that we are not. The shadow is an unconscious complex which is the diametrical opposite of the conscious self, the ego. The ego is everything we pretend that we are. The shadow contains everything that a person does not wish to consciously acknowledge within themselves. When Carl Jung talked about the shadow, he described it as having both a light and dark aspect. The warrior confronts the dark shadow first; the light shadow comes later. This is because facing the light shadow is more challenging than facing the dark shadow. Facing the dark shadow builds the foundation for working with the light.

The dark shadow is not evil: it is the container of all the stuff we threw out when we were growing up – everything we could not handle, everything we were told was wrong about us, everything we thought we could not be. A major difference between pseudo warriors and true warriors is that the former refuse to face their shadow. The warrior who has developed a strong centre of power can venture towards the shadow. Many myths deal with this very issue. There is the myth of Theseus who was guided by Ariadne through the labyrinth to meet and defeat the Minotaur. The story of Dr. Jekyll and Mr. Hyde also concerns the shadow. Here, a middle-aged scientist experiments with different potions and eventually transforms himself into a completely different person: an alter-ego, the animalistic Mr. Hyde. Hyde gradually gains more and more control over Jekyll. This is a story about the shadow. A story of right and wrong; joy and despair; good and evil. The story typifies the fear of facing the shadow. 'What if my worst side started to take over my better?' In consciously working with the shadow, this does not happen.

We are taught to be virtuous, to be kind, to be nice to people. But what do we do with the aspects of ourselves that we believe are not ok? If we are taught that strength is noble, what do we do with our vulnerability? If we are taught that courage is good, what do we do with our fear? If we are taught that academic success is good, what do we do with our emotions? The list is endless. Whenever we say one thing is good and another bad we become split beings; the part that is jettisoned becomes unconscious and the desired trait becomes more dominant in our consciousness. Looking out on the world and classifying things in terms of good and bad, right and wrong, is a recipe for a strong shadow. Some people try and kid themselves that they are love and light, others that they are sweet and polite. Anything not sweet and light then gets shamefully hidden away. Some people kid themselves that they are strong, hard and successful and they sweep everything soft and gentle in themselves into the unconscious.

Working with the shadow is not about being concerned with good or bad: it is about being whole. If we try to ditch our anger or our hate, we also risk ditching our passion and enthusiasm. When I met Colin, he could not get in touch with his passion. His spoke with a flat, monotonous voice and felt he had little direction in life. He had disowned his anger because he was afraid of it. He was afraid that, if he was angry, he would hurt people. So he did the easy thing and pushed it far away. It took a lot of work for Colin to dare to allow his anger to come to the surface. After he exploded with rage and beat several pillows to a pulp, he started to come alive. The anger was no longer hidden and dangerous but had come closer. His anger re-energized his whole being and his posture and voice became different as a result. As soon as he stopped being afraid of his anger, he could welcome it back.

Jan had learnt to disown her competitive side. She was a spiritual person who thought that chasing money was beneath her. She was not doing well financially. Her ability to make money was in her shadow. Some years later she was able to reclaim her competitive side. She not only was able to increase her income but she felt more alive as a result.

Francine was afraid of her hate. She had been taught that hate was bad and therefore could not allow herself to hate. Francine complained that she could not focus. She felt an intense hatred for her mother which confused her because she also felt love for her. As she stopped judging herself as being bad for hating her mother, she allowed the hatred to come closer. As she felt it course through her body she felt the tremendous focus that comes with strong, directed emotion. Hatred is not scattered; it is an emotion that can be directed with great intensity towards another person. As she welcomed her hatred, it began to change and inform her ability to focus and concentrate. Hatred often comes when a person feels that another consistently disregards their sense of identity, worth or boundary. Reclaiming her hatred helped Francine to be more assertive and draw clear boundaries.

The shadow becomes a tremendous ally when worked with consciously. When it remains unconscious, it feels like a powerful nemesis. Peter was a tough boss who was hated by his staff; they even made jokes about his 'fascist nature' behind his back. Yet, before he had accepted this particular management position, Peter had been quite mild by nature. In his previous post, good humour and reason worked very well; with this new post, the staff was of a different disposition and were used to confrontation with management. Peter soon started to feel a very different side of his nature rise to the fore, one that was more dynamic and aggressive. He felt split: on the one hand he was naturally gentle yet, on the other, he felt angry and frustrated at work and engaged in conflict readily. It was not until he left that job that he was able to integrate his aggressive shadow side. In his next management position, things were different. He had embraced his aggression and converted it into assertion. Now he was able to be both gentle and assertive as the need arose. Working with the shadow gave him a greater range of responses.

The shadow remains in the depths as long as we judge a quality within us as bad, defective, flawed or unacceptable. The person who regards the unconscious as a fearful repository of evil will have a strong shadow. The person who sees a world divided between forces of good and evil will have a strong shadow. When we suppress any feeling or impulse, we are suppressing some of our power. If we deny our ugliness, we lessen our beauty; if we deny our fear, we decrease our courage; and if we deny our hatred, we lessen our compassion. Facing the Shadow is about making peace with the contradictions that we find inside ourselves. Facing the shadow is the journey of understanding and reclaiming our projections.

Owning the Dark Shadow

What qualities in other people create an intense reaction in you?
What disgusts you about other people?
What frightens you about other people?
What enrages you about other people?
What things do you judge in other people?

Do you dislike people for being aggressive, arrogant, confused, dishonest, incongruent, petty, uncaring, unreasonable, or unthinking?

Do you judge politicians for being corruptible, soldiers for being violent, journalists for being blinkered or tyrants for being self-seeking?

Think of three people with whom you would least like to spend time. What qualities do these people have that you dislike?

The degree to which you are repulsed by these qualities is the degree to which you will suppress them in yourself and pretend that they are not within you.

Which emotions do you have difficulty in expressing?
Which emotions do you have difficulty with when others express them?

What are you most afraid of finding out about yourself?
Be honest with yourself.

It is only through being willing to own unpleasant qualities in yourself that you can begin to befriend your dark shadow and re-integrate its power.

Looking at the Shadow of Wealth

Do you find it easier to be in the company of wealthy or poor people?
Concerning the group you feel most uncomfortable with:
What judgements do you have around them?
What disgusts you about them?
What frightens you about them?
What enrages you about them?

If you have judgements about wealthy people, wealth lives in your shadow and needs to be reclaimed. Until this is done, you may feel afraid of being wealthy. The fear of gain will make happiness elusive.
Own your fears around having too much.

If you have judgements about poor people, poverty lives in your shadow and needs to be embraced. Until this is done, you may feel afraid of being poor and losing everything. The fear of loss will make happiness elusive.

Own your fears around having too little.

The shadow is a container of unconscious power. We need to face the shadow so that its energy can be returned to us. At first, facing the shadow can be uncomfortable because we have to acknowledge truths about ourselves that we would rather pretend were not so. When we realize that the shadow is not evil but our greatest friend, we can really integrate this unconscious power in a way that can change our lives. If we do not integrate this power, it gets stronger. In time, it may even start to destroy us. This is not because the shadow wants to hurt us, it is because our unconscious has become like a pressure cooker with no means of release. The build up of pressure will eventually lead to a terrible explosion.

There is an old story about a German hero called Siegfried who spent his youth in a blacksmith's shop. There, he forged a sword of such heroic properties that he could not be defeated in combat. With this sword in hand, Siegfried went in search of a mighty fire-breathing dragon that guarded a vast treasure. In heated combat, Siegfried slew the dragon and, while recovering his strength, he absently dipped his finger into the growing pool of blood flowing from the dragon and discovered that it was scalding hot. To cool his burning finger, he put it into his mouth. He was suddenly able to understand the language of the birds in the forest. The birds told him to bathe in the blood, because that would make his skin so tough that none of the weaponry of the times could pierce it and he did just that.

The dark shadow can appear as a scary dragon which we may try to avoid by running in the opposite direction, but it will follow us until we find the courage to turn and face it. Siegfried kills the dragon and its power begins to move and flow towards him through its blood. By tasting the blood, he assimilates some of this power so that nature begins to speak to him. When he fully immerses himself in the power of the dragon, he becomes invincible. He did not destroy the dragon: he merely liberated its power. We work with the shadow in the same way. We do not seek to destroy it. We seek to liberate it.

We recognize the shadow through our projections. Whenever we disown something like anger, aggression, fear, hatred, jealousy, or vulnerability we then throw it outside the self and see this trait in other people instead. They then become mirrors for our own disowned shadow. We do this because we pretend that the disowned quality has nothing to do with us. The person who believes that they are all love at heart yet looks out on to a world of great hate is likely to have pushed hate away into their shadow. The person who thinks that they are loyal and sees a world of betrayal is likely to have pushed betrayal away in their shadow. The person who thinks that they are compassionate but sees an uncaring world is likely to have pushed uncaring into their shadow. The external world that we see or feel is a clue to our inner world that we do not always see or feel. The person who has a disowned shadow will create division, conflict and scarcity around them.

The person who is conscious of their shadow feels empowered and open to a world of diversity and possibility. All energies inside the psyche need to be faced and embraced rather than denied or acted out unconsciously. If we refuse to confront and embrace the shadow, it will seek us out. If we run away, it will chase us. If we seek to protect ourselves, it will lay siege to the tower of the ego. The Tower card in the tarot deck represents just such an encounter. The tower that represents a restricted or naïve view of the world, an outdated self-image or an inappropriate value system has become a prison that needs to be broken open. We get used to our prisons and defend them because we believe in the adage 'better the devil you know'. The shadow holds the keys to our prison but we can get very frightened of this liberator. The shadow is not our enemy: it is our greatest ally.

The shadow is not something that we will face just once in our lives. Encountering it is an ongoing journey of self-realization. There is a myth of the Egyptian Sun God Ra who sailed across the heavens in the Barque of Millions of Years. During the midnight hour, the Sun God Ra was said to meet the greatest of all dangers, Apophis, the great snake of the night time sea. But Ra was aided each night by an unlikely ally, the God Seth who ruled over the desert and was considered the enemy of the Sun God by day. Each night, Seth would stand on the prow of the boat and defend the boat with his spear, allowing the barque to continue on its journey towards each sunrise. Each day we must make the journey of becoming more conscious. We must embrace our dark side so that we may journey through the light.

We work with the shadow through adopting a vigilant inner awareness. Dreams are one way in which to do this. In dreams, the shadow often appears through threatening or sinister figures such as gangsters, thieves, prostitutes, beggars, cheats or liars. Such dreams can be a gift, for through them the shadow comes nearer to consciousness.

Prosperity = The Gift of Mortality

Prosperity is about appreciating the true gift of life. The warrior is aware of the fragility and shortness of life and therefore seeks to live life to the full. Warriors are acutely aware that their time on the earth is limited. They do not take life for granted. For instance, no samurai sought to be safe from the shadow of death; indeed, they believed that they were already dead, it was just the sword had not yet struck.

Death walks with us through life. This may seem a morbid thought but acceptance of it can help us to live more fully. Many people have reported that a near miss with death, perhaps through an accident or illness, had helped them awaken to the beauty and mystery of life. Contemplating our death is a spiritual practice that helps us liberate our consciousness from trivial things. When our mortality is conscious, we can begin to view our lives with different eyes. Ask anyone suffering from a terminal disease and they will tell you how precious life is. To a person who has a short time to live, every moment becomes precious, every sunrise a miracle and every child a promise of the world's future. Death unites everyone on the planet, rich or poor, famous or ordinary, beggars or kings. The warrior is the hunter and the hunter is aware of the power of death. The contemplation of our mortality can even help us to wash the dishes with more presence and enthusiasm. To the warrior, death is a wise teacher who lets us know what is most important right now. Consciously facing death is a part of the hero's journey. If we can face our ultimate death, we can face all the little deaths that life brings. During our journey, different phases of our life will come and go. Youth will come and go but the person who is unafraid of death remains ever young at heart. Annihilation is our deepest fear, yet death is the natural order of things; it is a part of the cycle of life. Without death, there could be no new life.

Because we do not truly own our lives or anything else, prosperity is about stewardship, not the ownership principle of the scarcity game. Practising stewardship frees us from the fear of loss. How would you feel if you were to surrender all your money and your possessions and made your life's path more important? You are here on the earth for a limited time. What are you going to do with this gift of your precious life?

Honouring the Gift of Life

You will not live forever.
Imagine that you have six months to live.

What would you do with the remaining months of your life?
What places would you visit, what activities would you do?
From this perspective, how important is having money?

What would you like people to remember about your life?
What difference do you wish your life to make to others or to the planet?

Now imagine that you have one month to live.
What are your priorities now?

Chapter 12

Prosperity = A Kind of Magic

---

*Life is a marvellous adventure, a voyage of self-
discovery, a magically creative process.*

GILL EDWARDS

There is a story of a man who visited a remote Chinese village that was
suffering from extended drought. Although many prayers had been
offered to end the drought, nothing had worked. The people were
desperate and so they sent to a remote area for a well-respected
rainmaker. Soon, a wizened old man arrived in a cart. He alighted, sniffed
the air and asked for a cottage at the outskirts of the village. He insisted
that he not be disturbed and that his food be left outside his door. For
three days, the old man stayed alone in the cottage. On the fourth day, the
village awoke to a downpour of rain mixed with snow which was
unheard of that time of year.

The visitor was greatly impressed and spoke with the old man. 'So you
can make it rain?'

The old man replied, 'Of course I cannot.'

'But there was a persistent drought until you came,' the visitor
objected. 'Oh, that is something quite different. I come from a region
where everything is in order, it rains when it should and it is fine when it
is needed, and the people are also in order in themselves. But that was not
the case with the people here; they were out of Tao and out of
themselves. I was at once affected when I arrived, so I had to be quite
alone until I was once more with the Tao and then it naturally rained.'

Principle Twelve   *Prosperity is about energy flow. Through being in
harmony with our personal energy flow and with
cosmic flow we can build a heaven on earth. This
is the way of the magician.*

Prosperity = A Magical Way

Prosperity is a magical art. Magic is the art of creating change in the world through the power of our consciousness. Magic is not only in the universe, it is in us. We can create what we want on the earth. We must just believe it is possible, then do a little work to manifest what we want on the earth.

The word 'magician' derives from the Indo-European root word magh, meaning 'to be able' and 'to have power'. One of the earliest images of a human being is the so-called 'Sorcerer' in the Palaeolithic cave of Les Trois Freres in southern France. He stands presiding over a swarm of bison, ibex, bear, deer, and mammoth painted on the stone slabs below him. Similar magical figures appear in cave paintings of the Early European Tribes of about 18,000 years ago. The magician was present at the beginnings of human society, and flourished in ancient Egypt, Greece, and the Middle East, as well as in India and China.

For thousands of years, shamans and Holy Ones have worked with the power of the universe to heal lack and to generate abundance. They know how to call upon this power to manifest vitality and good health, and all kinds of good things such as rain, sunshine or an abundant food supply. They can do this because they know that this power flows through all things – through a song, a rainbow, a flock of migrating birds in flight, a mountain, a group of people, and the earth itself. It is this sense of interconnectedness that the shaman or magician works with in order to manifest. This is very different from believing that the power in the universe is separate from all created things. It is a different way than asking an external deity to answer our prayers. This is a key point in understanding magic of any kind; magic works because it is already inside of each one of us, we have simply forgotten this amazing fact.

The power of the universe flows through all things. All living creatures are connected to this power yet, for the most part, human beings living in the modern world do not experience this. People disconnect their lives from this power by enclosing themselves within a world of concrete, plastic, technology and rationality. Reconnecting with this power can be as simple as taking your shoes off and walking on the warm, bare earth, standing under the stars and gazing at their beauty, or sitting before a flower and feeling the life force that flows through its delicate form. Everything alive has power; if it did not, it would no longer be alive. To be alive means to be connected to the life force that flows through all things. If you are alive and have a pulse, you can take it that you are connected to the power of the universe. Learning to work with this power can take a lifetime of exploration. Magic is a path of ecstasy, not theology and magicians have called upon this power through singing, play, humour, and simple ritual rather than through dry intellectual debate or posturing. Magic has long been an art that has avoided doctrine and commandments and has instead embraced activities such as poetry and dance. Magic is about joy and ecstasy, and it sees little value in mindless suffering.

Power has long been used for healing. Jack Schwarz, author of *The Power of Personal Health* (Arkana, 1992), discovered at an early age that he had healing power. When WWII broke out, he was seventeen and he joined the Dutch Resistance. He was captured, imprisoned and tortured by the Nazis, but they were baffled by his ability to heal his wounds one after another. After the war had finished, he was tested in the U.S. by medical doctors and scientists for his incredible ability to control his physical and psycho-neural capacities. Under laboratory conditions, he was able to demonstrate his ability to stick long needles through his arm and feel no pain. Sometimes the needles were infected with viruses or bacteria yet he showed no trace of subsequent infection. Jack Schwarz's comment on his amazing abilities was that he simply knew how to attune his consciousness to the power of the universe.

Olga Kharitidi, a Russian doctor and psychiatrist, worked for some years in Soviet mental hospitals. Her orthodox views of health, and reality, were challenged by her unlooked-for experiences with the living shamanic traditions of the snowbound Altai Mountains of Siberia. Subsequently, Dr. Kharitidi began applying some shamanic methods to her own patients, presenting them to her colleagues as scientific experiments. She was so moved by the results that she went on to write and teach about shamanism. She now works on exploring alternative methods of healing for people suffering with deep trauma.[1]

Magic can be used to heal or harm. Just as electricity can light a house or kill someone, so can universal power be used creatively or destructively. A friend of mine, Alberto Villoldo, tells the story of visiting Haiti as a graduate student and encountering the healing philosophy and practices of Voodoo. Being a young man and scientifically minded at the time, he found this whole concept of magic hard to believe. He did not believe that magic could be used to harm or heal and he was sure that magic only worked for those that believed in it. He made a hundred dollar wager with a fellow anthropologist that Voodoo could not affect him. He was taken to meet an old Voodoo priest who turned to Alberto, laughing loudly and saying in broken English, 'You want to believe?' The agreement was that the priest would do his work on the following Monday, by which time Alberto would have returned to California. At the appointed time, he was having dinner with friends and telling them about the bet. He expected nothing to happen and he was not disappointed. He was also fine the next day and the day after but on the third day he developed a headache that turned into a migraine. By the evening, he was having intestinal spasms and began to retch uncontrollably. At midnight the phone rang and his anthropologist friend rang from Haiti saying that they had been unable to work on the Monday, as agreed, and that he had just returned from a Voodoo ceremony and wanted to know if Alberto was feeling anything.[2]

Black magic is anything that deliberately harms or hinders another. Black magic may work at one level but, at a higher level, it is a huge mistake. Attempting to direct power towards destructive ends has consequences. The web of power is guarded by the principle of Karma which says 'as you sow, so shall you reap.' This is why black magicians are notorious for not living very long lives. This is why it is wise to work with power for your own upliftment and for the upliftment of others.

Magic is about using power. Many philosophies teach that we are relatively powerless in the face of objective reality. They say that we exist in a universe determined either by the laws of physics, or by our genetic inheritance, or by our past, luck, karma, fate, or by the whims of some spiritual hierarchy. Most people do not believe that they have any power to influence external reality. Life then becomes something that just happens rather than something that is actively participated in. Magic is a philosophy that believes in something radically different. From the Druids of Ancient Britain to the Kahunas of Hawaii to the Shamans of South America to the Wise Ones of Africa, every culture without exception has had a long and beneficial relationship with magic. Magic is the most ancient of philosophies. Magic says that all the people, situations, dilemmas and paradoxes we meet – our external reality – are mirror images of our internal world of thought, belief, choice, feeling and emotion. If our inner energy landscape is one where weeds of confusion have been allowed to grow, or where seeds of resentment and regret have been allowed to flourish, then our outer reality will reflect that perfectly. If our inner landscape is one of volcanic anger that has been suppressed to the point of explosion, our outer reality will reflect that too. If we have cultivated and nurtured our emotional energies, and allowed expression, these will also be reflected in our outer world.

The Hermetic tradition of Ancient Egypt states it, 'As above so below, as within so without.' This goes far beyond cause and effect. Our vibration will act like a magnet to attract similar energies in the outside world. It will similarly repel incompatible energies. The person who feels fear as a core way of moving through the world will start to attract a similar vibration. This vibration of fear may manifest in any number of ways. It can come in the form of a bully or persecutor who also vibrates with fear. A person who resonates with gratitude and blessings will start to attract a similar vibration; they will find that they start to attract the things for which they are grateful. Resentment will attract things that evoke further resentment. It is a vicious or blessed circle depending on where you are standing. Just as a certain vibration attracts so it can repel: a person vibrating hatred will repel love; a person vibrating desperation will repel fulfilment; and a person vibrating abundance will repel lack.

Prosperity = The Rainbow Walk

Magic comes from understanding and using our inner power. Each of us has a number of energy centres called chakras. These energy centres are vortices of light that are not to be found in the physical but in the subtle body, along the area that corresponds with the main nerve ganglia of the spinal column. They are sometimes also referred to as lotus flowers because they grow out of the mud and face the light of the heavens. These chakras hold the patterns of the psyche that attract or repel possible experiences. From these centres, we intimately weave the patterns of prosperity or scarcity. The word chakra comes from ancient Sanskrit and means 'wheel' or 'disc'. The magician works with these energy centres to build a rainbow bridge to connect heaven and earth in a great vibrating channel of light.

Base Chakra – Survive and Thrive

This centre is located at the perineum. It relates to our survival instincts and to our sense of gravity, grounding and connection to our bodies and to the earth. Its Sanskrit name, *Muladhara*, means 'root' or 'support'. A balanced base chakra leads to our feeling stable and secure on the earth. Its colour is red and its elemental force is earth. This is the centre of our physical identity, the foundation of our whole system. Here is located our fight or flight response and all impulses that deal with self-preservation. The base chakra deals with our material and monetary existence. When open and functioning as it should, it brings vitality, a sense of security, and dynamic presence. This centre deals with the power to have.

A person with an over-charged base chakra may be a hoarder, greedy, and a spendthrift. They can be workaholics and fixated on material things. People with a weak base may feel deep insecurity and even have a desire to escape physical life altogether. People who think of the earth as evil will shut down the base chakra. People who have money difficulties and who find it difficult to be or survive in the world usually have some kind of problem in this chakra. People who feel that they have no home on the earth and wander from place to place may have base chakra issues. People who are raised in families with strong scarcity issues tend to have weak base chakras. People with a weak base chakra feel disconnected from the earth. One of the main reasons why we experience so much scarcity is because of our disconnected relationship to the earth.

> Enjoy and celebrate your body and its connection to nature. Stand in front of trees, sit in gardens, exercise and dance on the bare earth. Notice the colour red around you. Experiment with wearing the colour red. Breathe, eat and walk consciously. Be more aware of all your daily dealings with money.

Sacral Chakra - Celebrate and Enjoy

This centre relates to feeling, desire, pleasure and sensation. Its Sanskrit name, *Svadhisthana*, means 'sweetness'. It is located in the lower abdomen, below the navel. Its colour is orange and its elemental force is water. This is the seat of our emotional and sexual identity; because of this, it is often called the seat of life. When open, it brings a sense of fluidity, fulfilment, depth of feeling, and the ability to accept change. It is our nature to desire things, whether that be food, shelter, warmth, love, enjoyment, or meaning. From desire comes passion and passion is a force that seeks to flow out into the world. The sacral chakra is the centre of pleasure which, when followed, consciously leads to a more prosperous life. The body needs sensuous touch, and the emotions need to be felt and expressed. A fully functioning sacral chakra opens a person both to acknowledging the pleasures of life and also to a full range of feeling.

A person with excess energy in the sacral chakra may have sexual addictions and obsessive relationships; they can also suffer from mood swings. This can be the result of a repression of emotions and desires leading to a tremendous constriction of energy. Energy that is repressed is usually acted upon unconsciously. This leads to pain and suffering. Considerable suffering in the world is generated through the unconscious use of sexual energy. The global population crisis is fuelled by a lack of awareness and consciousness of sexual energy. A person with a depleted sacral centre may feel a lack of desire, an absence of passion and may avoid pleasure. A balanced centre leads to emotional intelligence.

> Enjoy, celebrate and express your emotions and desires. Follow them consciously. Make everything you do a meditation on pleasure and sensuality. Allow yourself to follow what you truly desire and consciously open to the delights of physical, emotional and mental pleasure. Notice the colour orange around you. Experiment with wearing this colour.

Solar Plexus Chakra: Influence and Shape

This centre governs our metabolism, sense of personal power, will, and self-determination. Its Sanskrit name, *Manipura*, means 'lustrous jewel'. The colour of this centre is yellow and its elemental force is fire. This is the centre of our ego identity. This is the centre that seeks to define who we are and put boundaries around our identity and possessions. When open and flowing, it generates a field of effectiveness, spontaneity, and non-dominating power. Here is found the will power to break out of self-limiting patterns. In this centre, we begin to understand that we are the creators of our destiny and we can influence and shape the world around us. Will is the power that breaks through inertia. Will helps us to know what we want and moves us towards new horizons. This is the centre of the warrior.

People with an overactive solar centre can be abusive, bullying, controlling, dominating, overbearing, stubborn or arrogant. A depleted centre generates passivity, low self-esteem, poor self-discipline and irresponsibility. Problems in this chakra have led to countless wars and much pain and hardship. A balanced centre leads to confidence, playfulness and vitality.

> Enjoy, celebrate and express your will and intent. Make consciously following your goals and taking risks a daily practice. Give space to others. Silently refute invalidation of any kind. Fight for rather than against. Let go of attachment to results. Notice the colour yellow around you. Experiment with wearing this colour.

Heart Chakra: Connect and Love

This is the centre of love, connection and relating. It is the place in which we integrate opposites in the psyche: mind and body; male and female; ego and shadow; spirit and matter. Its Sanskrit name, *Anahata*, means 'unstruck'. This is the seat of our social identity. It is located in the heart region and its colour is either pink or green. When open and healthy, we can feel compassion, love and a sense of centredness. The heart is where we resolve the dilemma between initiative and guilt. In this centre, we can feel a deep sense of unity with all things and a sense of real peace. It has been said that 'relationships are the Yoga of the West'. Relationship is the way of the heart centre. Community nurtures the heart, as do all truly loving relationships. Love is highly magnetic and draws all good things to a person.

The person with too much energy in the heart centre is the classic giver who finds it hard to receive. This is the energy state of the pleaser and the co-dependent. A deficient heart centre leads to anti-social behaviour, feelings of alienation, disconnection and loneliness. A balanced centre creates acceptance, peace and contentment.

> Enjoy, celebrate and express your serenity and love for yourself and others. Make compassion for yourself and others a daily meditation. Look to the community of your heart. Consciously build a network of support and nurturing. Give and receive consciously. Notice the colours pink and green around you. Experiment with wearing these colours at different times.

Throat Chakra: Express and Create

This centre relates to sound, communication, self-expression, and vibration. It is the centre of our creative identity. Its colour is bright cerulean blue. The Sanskrit name of the throat centre is *Vishuddha* which means 'purification'. The throat chakra is the centre that processes pure vibration. The Hindus believe that vibration creates every level of the manifest universe. When the throat chakra is open, a person becomes aware of the universe around as pure vibration. Our voice is the living expression of our vibrational existence in the world. Opening this chakra means that we also start to attune to the gentle voice of spirit. In this centre we hear the whispers that call us ever onwards towards higher consciousness. As we awaken the throat, we also open to speaking our own truth regardless of what others may say or think. This is the centre of the true creative artist, whether that creativity manifests as a drawing, a painting or grounding an idea or creating a business.

An overactive throat chakra can lead to talking too much, excessive loudness, and difficulty in keeping silent or confidentiality. A deficient throat chakra can lead to a fear of speaking, shyness, and problems in self-expression and articulation. A balanced centre leads to living a creative and expressive life.

Enjoy, celebrate and express your inner authenticity, integrity and truth. Make speaking the unspeakable a daily practice. Sing often. Actively pursue creativity in the world. Notice the colour sky blue around you. Experiment with wearing this colour.

Third Eye Chakra: Imagine and Flow

This is the centre of inner sight, imagination, clairvoyance and sensing light and colour. Its Sanskrit name, Ajna, means 'to know, perceive or command'. The third eye chakra is located in the middle of the head behind the forehead. Its colour is indigo blue. This is the centre of our mythic or archetypal identity. An open third eye allows a person to reflect upon and see into the hidden patterns of life. When awakened, this centre helps a person to imagine, daydream, envision, focus and see the light in all things. This is the centre of the dreamer and disciplined meditator.

An over-stimulated third eye leads to delusions, illusions, excessive fantasizing, wild night dreams, and even hallucinations. An under-stimulated third eye can lead to a lack of vision and imagination and an inability to see the way forward. A balanced centre allows good memory recall and opens the way for intuition and deep insight to blossom.

Enjoy, celebrate and express your visions, insights and wisdom. Look for the vibrancy and colour of life. Make it a practice to imagine a light-filled present and a glorious future. Notice the colour deep blue around you. Experiment with wearing this colour.

Crown Chakra: Consciousness and Bliss

This centre relates to thinking, consciousness, the timeless dimension of spirit, and higher wisdom. Its Sanskrit name, Sahasrara, means 'thousand-fold'. The crown chakra is the centre of our spiritual identity; Hindus believe that it is the centre of enlightenment. Its natural psychological state is one of transcendent bliss. This is the culmination of the whole chakra system. The lotus that started in the mud of the base chakra is now blossoming into the thousand-petalled flower. When open, this centre is one of higher consciousness and also a gateway to higher intelligence. The crown chakra is the centre of pure knowing beyond reason and of mystical consciousness.

An over-stimulated crown centre can generate feelings of confusion, disassociation and over-intellectualizing. It can also lead to spiritual mania. A deficient crown centre can cause cynicism about spiritual matters, and a disconnection from spirit. A balanced centre leads to self-realization and spiritual mastery.

Enjoy, celebrate and express your spirituality and inner wisdom. Make silence a daily practice. Explore the power of stillness and presence. Notice the colour violet around you. Experiment with wearing this colour.

Soul Star: Cosmic Identity

This chakra sits somewhere between eighteen inches and two feet above the crown centre. This is the centre of our universal identity. It is the place from which we open to divine love and spiritual selflessness. When open, it can lead to out-of-body travel, advanced dream-recall capabilities, and healing gifts. This chakra holds the blueprint for the whole chakra system and, in turn, the physical body. When this centre awakens, a larger unseen reality becomes apparent.

There is no excessive or deficient tendency for this chakra; it is either consciously realized or remains unknown and unfelt. This chakra awakens in time in those who are on a spiritual path of growth.

Enjoy, celebrate and express your connection to the cosmos. Dwell daily on the thought that you are a being of light, a child of the stars, and that you have come to fulfil a spiritual purpose on the earth. Notice the colour gold around you. Experiment with wearing this colour.

Prosperity = Balance and Harmony

Prosperity is about balance and harmony. Working with the chakras is about bringing the whole system into alignment and flow. Sometimes, one or two chakras need some work in order to bring back a feeling of wholeness and aliveness. Sometimes the work is about enlivening a particular centre and sometimes about releasing energy from it.

Michael approached me during a seminar on energy healing. He complained of not feeling that he had a home on the earth; he was shortly moving out of where he was staying and was not sure where he was going to live, nor even if he would continue living in the same country. He was also having difficulties around work and money. I told him that these were classic base chakra issues. I advised him to ground himself by walking in nature and doing some gentle physical exercise. I also suggested that wearing red occasionally might help. I am not sure how he is doing but I hope he feels more settled on the earth.

Stephen felt closed to feeling any real pleasure in life. His sexual energy was almost non-existent. He had grown up with an invasive mother and had learnt to close down as a means of protecting himself. Because this was a deep issue, it took a while for him to open his sacral chakra. He did a lot of work on connecting to his repressed emotions and desires. With persistence he was able to release a lot of anger and sadness about his upbringing. He made acknowledging and following his passions a daily exercise. Slowly, like a delicate flower, his sacral centre opened. During this process, Stephen felt that he was able to re-live some of his 'unlived adolescence'.

Rachel often felt that other people pushed her around and disregarded her boundaries. She worked on her solar chakra to build up more inner power and confidence to move through the world. She meditated on breathing sunlight into the solar centre each morning. She also started to go dancing. After just a few weeks, she started to feel a real difference. Gradually, she felt more 'radiant' and was increasingly able to be more protective of her own space.

Adam felt alone in life. As he worked on the heart chakra in meditation, he felt layers of pain on issues of betrayal surfacing. When he was younger, one of his elder brothers had violently assaulted him and this had left him with an energetic scar in his heart chakra. After some months of working on this issue through meditation and other work, he felt able to trust people a little more. As his heart healed, he realized that the incident with his brother was an isolated one. He found compassion in his heart for his brother, whom he realized must have been in a lot of pain himself at the time. As he forgave and let go of this past hurt, he no longer felt so held back in his relating with others.

Amanda was not able to express her emotions or herself very easily. She felt 'strangled' in life. She started to work on her throat chakra and took regular singing classes and individual lessons to open her voice. She also had some counselling to help her gain some insight into what was stopping her from expressing her feelings. In time, she gained both insight and the tools to find her authentic voice. She received consistent feedback that she had a lovely singing voice. She went on to lead chanting and creative voice workshops.

Anna felt that she had a morbid imagination. She did not like to do creative visualization exercises because she saw 'dark images' which frightened her. She had far too much energy in her third eye which needed to be discharged. She was too open to picking up energy from other people. She had 'energy cords' connecting her third eye to other members of her family. These needed to be dissolved by visualizing light flowing through them. She needed to let go of connecting to other people in this way. As she cleared her third eye of other people's energy, Anna came to know and trust her own energy all the more. She found that she had a great imagination and a naturally creative talent for visualizing. As she engaged her imagination towards the things she wanted, her life completely changed. She changed her job for one that was more in line with her creative abilities. She moved home to an area for which she had a stronger affinity. She now feels more on track in her life and more in the driving seat of her destiny.

Michael had been interested in spirituality from a young age but received the message from his parents and from others that this was not a normal pursuit for someone so young. When he was seventeen years old, he decided to follow a 'normal' life. By the time he was thirty-two, he was desperately unhappy and practically suicidal. By chance he met someone who introduced him to a series of spiritual books. An old, familiar fire raged inside him. When Michael was young, he had an awakened crown chakra. People around him did not understand him and he shut down. Now in his thirties, he was able to find people interested in spirituality and was able to open to the wisdom of the crown chakra. This wisdom helped him to move forward both spiritually and materially. He has since trained as a coach. He connects with the wisdom of his crown chakra to receive intuitive information to help his clients move forward.

Soul Star Cleansing

Sit quietly and focus on your breathing.

Close your eyes and imagine yourself in a beautiful landscape.

Above you is a golden sun. Imagine standing beneath this sun; this is your soul star chakra. Invite its light to wash through you. Immediately, golden light pours down over you like a great waterfall of light. Just imagine that you can let go of any old or stuck energy in your energy centres; feel them being washed clean.

Imagine that this light starts to flow through you as well. Feel this light cleansing your bones, blood and all the cells of your body. Imagine sending this cleansing light to all your money. Imagine sending this cleansing light to the money passing through your bank account. Imagine sending this cleansing light to everything you own.

When you are ready, thank your soul star and allow the waterfall of light gradually to stop.

Take a few long, slow breaths and come back to waking consciousness.

Personal Sacred Space

Always start by sitting or lying in a quiet space. Relax your body and start to take some long, slow, conscious breaths.

Ground into the earth by imagining roots growing out of your feet or the base of your spine and pushing down on each out breath. Send these roots right down to the core of the earth.

Imagine breathing up energy from the core of the earth. Breathe it up into your base chakra and allow this energy to open the red bud into a fully blooming flower. Then breathe the energy up into the sacral, then the solar, and then the heart centres. Take your time breathing energy up into each.

Then imagine sending threads of energy out from your crown chakra on each out breath. Send these energy threads right up to the heart of the sun.

Imagine breathing energy down from the sun. Breathe it down to the crown chakra and allow this energy to open the violet flower into a fully blooming flower. Then breathe the energy down into the third eye, and the throat and then the heart centres.

In the heart, you now have a meeting place of earth and cosmic energy. Begin to breathe both of these energies into the heart until it begins to glow with energy. Allow your heart energy to expand until it surrounds your whole body in an egg of light.

Imagine a protective symbol – such as a cross, a five pointed star, a six pointed star, or an ankh (if you cannot imagine a protective symbol then use the image of a red rose) – and imagine placing this symbol before your heart centre. Place this symbol behind you, to the left and right, above and below you also. See that every direction has a protective symbol. Then place this symbol within your heart.

Take some long, slow breaths and come back to waking consciousness.

Energizing a Deficiency

Always start by sitting or lying in a quiet space. Relax your body and start to take some long, slow, conscious breaths.

Ground into the earth by imagining roots growing out of your feet or the base of your spine and pushing down on each out breath. Send these roots right down to the core of the earth. Then imagine sending threads of energy out from your crown chakra on each out breath. Send these energy threads right up to the heart of the sun.

Imagine energy flowing up from the earth for several in breaths and up to the sun on the out breath. Then change the direction and imagine energy flowing down from the sun for several in breaths and down into the earth on the out breath.

Then focus on the deficient centre; see it as a flower that is slowly opening and imagine breathing energy either up from the earth or down from the sun into this centre. Imagine that this centre is able to store this energy and that is begins to glow like a radiant light. Keep doing this until this centre feels energized.

As a separate exercise, you could also try breathing a colour into this centre to energize it. You can try vibrant colours such as tangerine orange, ruby red, bright gold, sapphire blue or emerald green.

Take some long, slow breaths and come back to waking consciousness.

Releasing an Excess of Energy

Always start by sitting or lying in a quiet space. Relax your body and start to take some long, slow, conscious breaths.

Ground into the earth by imagining roots growing out of your feet or the base of your spine and pushing down on each out breath. Send these roots right down to the core of the earth. Then imagine sending threads of energy out from your crown chakra on each out breath. Send these energy threads right up to the heart of the sun.

Imagine energy flowing up from the earth for several in breaths and up to the sun on the out breath. Then change the direction and imagine energy flowing down from the sun for several in breaths and down into the earth on the out breath.

Then focus on the centre and see it as a flower that is about to open. Imagine breathing out energy from it and sending it either down to the earth or up to the sun. Imagine that you can release excess energy held in this centre.

Imagine that you can release anyone else's energy from this centre on the out breath. If you sense that you have energy cords connecting you to other people, imagine sending light down these cords and ask that the light dissolve them.

As a separate exercise, you could also try breathing a colour into this centre to help in harmonizing it. Soothing colours may work best, such as pale amethyst, diamond white light, light yellow or a gentle pink.

Take some long slow breaths and come back to waking consciousness.

Prosperity = The Magic of Resonance

We create our own reality. We do this from the core of our being, from the inside out. Our core tone is the music that we play to the universe. It is the frequency to which the world responds. Our orchestra consists of the musical notes of the chakras. Every chakra is both a receiver and transmitter of energy. Therefore, each chakra is potentially a powerful centre of manifestation.

First and foremost, we must know how to meet the basic demands of our physical selves. We need to know how to pay the rent and keep our lives in good repair. Prosperity is like a strong tree with deep roots into the earth. The deeper we feel connected to the earth, the taller we can reach into the heavens. Thus having a solid base chakra gives us a foundation from which we can build a prosperous life. For anyone who feels less than solid on the earth, the base chakra is the place to work. This means spending time in nature, enjoying the elements and getting more physical with life.

Emotions and desires of the sacral chakra are the fuel for manifesting what we want. If we do not desire something or feel a pleasant emotion associated with it, we will not strive for it. Passion is the powerhouse of manifesting.

Our will is the driving force behind knowing our dreams. When the will is connected to the vision of the third eye, we become unstoppable.

Many people are strongly centred in the heart and, even if they cannot visualize very well, they are able to feel what they want here. The vibration of love is the strongest force in the universe. It is stronger than fear. A person vibrating with love, appreciation and compassion will create miracles around them.

The throat is one of the most powerful centres for manifesting. 'In the beginning was the word.' Some indigenous tribes believe that the world was created through song. Working with sound is a whole science in itself. Each chakra has a tone; the throat has the power to activate all of the other chakras. Our words are highly creative. When we speak our authentic truth, others will hear the power of our words. The throat chakra gives us the power to say 'yes' and 'no' in life. We must choose to use this power wisely.

The third eye helps us to see where we want to head in life and what we want. When a person has a strong grounding on the earth, an activated will, and is willing to follow the vision of their third eye, then they are a dream-weaver, a certain kind of magician that has the power to turn intangible dreams into realities.

The crown connects us to the wisdom of our higher self; here, we connect to the wisdom beyond the self and are guided on our path. The person who has an awakened crown and is connected both to heaven and earth allows synchronicity and miracles to happen.

Shamans have long held the view that we dream our personal and collective worlds into being; they believe that this world is simply a grand drama or illusion created by consciousness. This means that time and space are illusions and that we can learn to dream a new dream. In all magical traditions there is the concept that consciousness is able to influence, move, shape, and weave reality into being. All spiritual traditions teach that everything manifests on a spiritual level before manifesting on the physical. Stories that come from the Bible, from the Kabala, and from various Taoist, Hindu, yogic, alchemical, Egyptian, and shamanic works show that miracles were once an everyday occurrence. The tool of the light-worker is imagination, which acts as both a gateway and a bridge to the realms of energy and this world. The key is to visualize the end result and not be too concerned about the process. If you state the outcome, the universe will work out all the details.

Sarah knew from a young age that she wanted to be in the world of theatre. She was just twelve when she first saw a video of the making of the highly successful play *Miss Saigon*. She instantly fell in love with the lead part. Being part Philippino and part English, she had the right look, but more importantly, she had a feeling that the role was right for her, and a strong sense of self-belief and trust. She daily visualized herself playing the lead role as she sang the songs from the show. A friend managed to get her an audition for the show at the tender age of fourteen and she so impressed the director that he told her to come back in a year's time. When she was seventeen, she landed a part in the London West End show. Two years later, she was singing the lead role of Kim in Sweden. Five years later, Sarah used the same technique of visualization to get the lead role of Princess Anjuli in the West End show *Far Pavilions*. Sarah says that 'these parts felt like they were almost dropped down from heaven for me.' Sarah is one of those imaginative and magical people that can be found working in the theatre.

Isabel, another talented actress, learned the technique of visualizing golden light around herself and other people. When she went to auditions, she would send a golden light to everyone taking part. After doing this for some weeks, she landed a job working in an advert selling a product that had gold as a major aspect of its brand. The advertisements paid her very handsomely for nearly two years.

Andrew was passionate about different forms of alternative healing. He fell in love with a certain modality of energy healing that was very expensive. The equipment and energy products on offer cost hundreds and even thousands of pounds. He had experimented with visualization over the years and decided to give it a go again. Every night he imagined having all the energy products that he wanted. Within a couple of months, someone in the organization approached Andrew, asking him if he would store some of the products in London for them. In return, he would be loaned some products on an indefinite basis. He agreed and was loaned around £15,000 worth of products and was also given nearly £4,000 worth as a gift by a friend.

Esther has a passion for shoes. Not just any old shoes: her penchant is for Jimmy Choo shoes, an expensive luxury brand worn by A-list celebrities. She long dreamed of owning a pair, but they were far beyond her humble budget. She attended a talk by an inspirational speaker who talked about 'thoughts becoming things'. She visited the speaker's website and was invited to sign up to its daily newsletter. Before she could sign up for the newsletter, she had to enter three wishes. She entered her wish for 'a pair of sparkly Jimmy Choos'. She received the newsletter which said, 'Fear not. Having set your intention, the Choos are now on their way to you,' and 'Boy, just visualize how great those Choos are gonna look on you!' She chuckled at the emails and enjoyed playing along, thinking about her Choos, and getting excited by the fact that, somehow, they were heading in her direction. A few months later, she was changing jobs and the company she was leaving threw a party for her. Towards the end of the evening, she was presented with a parcel. She tore off a piece of the wrapping paper and spotted one word, 'Choo', in all its distinguished, silver-lettered glory. Her fingers (and heart rate) sped up, the remaining wrapping paper flew all over the place, she opened the box and... imagine her joy as, at long last, she came face to face with her very own (extremely sparkly) pair of Jimmy Choo shoes.

Cate is an artist who loved the film *The Matrix*. She decided that it would be a cool thing to go to the premier of the sequel in the West End.

Although she had no way of going, she sat down with her mother and lit a candle with the intention of being there. She visualized herself going to the premiere all week. A couple of days later, she was invited to a dinner where she met one of the financiers of the film. She told him of her dream and he said that he would see what he could do. On the day of the film premier, Cate had a phone call. The guy she met at the party had a spare ticket after a friend dropped out at the last minute. Cate had her wish and also had a great time.

After training as an NLP Practitioner, I came across a visualizing technique that I enjoyed very much. The visualization involved travelling along a road to visit the past and future. I used a BMW sports car for the visualization. Although this was not the focus of the visualization, about six weeks later I was given a BMW sports car. The only difference between the visualized car and the one that turned up in the outside world was that the former was red and the latter silver. After driving it around for a while I discovered that I preferred silver!

Visualize What You Want

Spend 5 to 10 minutes every day visualizing what you want. Early mornings and evenings are good times to do this exercise.

Imagine the house in which you would like to live, the kind of neighbourhood, the kind of work you would like to do, the things you would love to do with your leisure time and so on.

One key to working with visualization is that it should be done in short and intense bursts. When the visualization has been done, it should then be released. Like drawing a bow at the highest point of tension, the arrow is released.

Once the inner work is done, it should be completely released. Do not even think about it again until the time comes round for the work to be repeated. Repetition is useful until it is no longer helpful. You will recognize the difference through practise.

Scattering Golden Blessings

Spend a minute sitting in silence. Feel your connection to the earth below and the sun above.

Breathe a golden light into your body; imagine that your whole aura is super charged with this golden light. Then, throughout the day, imagine sending golden light to other people and situations to bless them. Imagine that this golden light is a blessing of prosperity. Experiment with other colours, such as fuchsia pink for love and passion, turquoise blue for creativity and so on.

Bless others and open to being blessed yourself from unexpected sources.

Soul Star Manifesting

Spend a minute sitting in silence. Feel your connection to the earth below.

Then imagine the soul star above your head. See it blazing like a radiant golden sun. Imagine that its golden light is surrounding you in an egg of light.

Then spend 5 to 10 minutes visualizing what you want.

Then imagine surrendering this vision up to the soul star chakra.

Gradually, imagine the Soul Star withdrawing its light and disappearing from view.

Take a few deep breaths and come back to waking consciousness.

References
1. Kharitidi, Olga. Entering the Circle. HarperSanFrancisco, 1997
2. Villoldo, Alberto. Shaman, Healer, Sage. Bantam, 2001

Chapter 13

Prosperity = Embracing Infinity

In my soul there is a temple, a shrine,
a mosque, a church where I kneel.

RABIA AL ADAWIYA

There is a story of a man who dies and crosses between this world and the next and comes to a place of great light. An angel of shimmering light greets him there and offers to give him a tour of Heaven. The man is thrilled and enjoys the tour until the angel says, 'That is your room but I do not want to show it to you because it is so sad!' The man is curious and asks the angel to show him. Eventually, the angel agrees and opens the door. The man is amazed for the room is full of material riches, jewels, money, gold and sumptuous different coloured cloth. 'Why is it a sad room?' asks the man. 'Because these are the things that God constantly tried to give you but you refused to accept them.'

Principle Thirteen *Prosperity is about living happily on the earth. When we embrace polarities and paradox, we open the way to living blissfully. This is the way of the divine lover.*

Prosperity = The Way of the Lover

Prosperity is a cosmic dance. According to the philosophy of the Tao, life is a great cosmic interplay between yin and yang, feminine and masculine. This is the playground of the lover. The way of the lover involves embracing opposites: innocence and pleasure; intimacy and aloneness; heart and mind; prosperity and scarcity; spirit and matter. Prosperity comes from the sacred dance between the masculine and feminine. Scarcity comes when there is a war between them. For centuries, scarcity has raised masculine yang energy to an honoured platform and has debased and insulted feminine yin energy. Feminine energy has been believed to be inferior to masculine energy. This has created vast suffering across the planet for centuries, if not thousands of years.

In the paradigm of scarcity, both women and men suffer. Scarcity has created many stereotypes around gender that hinder people's becoming whole and happy. The media constantly produce powerful imagery of what men and women should look like and act like. Men are supposed to look powerful and rugged and be hard. Such men love women and then leave them. Such women are supposed to look glamourous and sexy and be soft. These women attract men and then do anything to keep them. Men are encouraged to be 'real' men and women 'real' women. This nonsense perpetuates unhappy relationships and has created generations of confusion and misery.

It is a principle of consciousness and energy that the yin and the yang will ever desire to seek each other out. There is an old Arabic story of a beautiful young boy called Qays. He was aged ten when he began school and met the young girl Layla. He was struck by her beauty. Her hair was as dark as night and even her name derived from a word meaning 'night' in Arabic. They were both love-struck. Soon others noticed, and tongues began to wag. Qays was forced to stop seeing her; this broke his heart and he slipped into melancholy and then into madness. He started to wander the land chanting poems of his love for Layla. Layla also held on to her love for Qays in the secret chamber of her heart. She heard her lover's voice through every child that sang his verses, through every passer-by that hummed one of his love-songs. She thus lived between the water of her tears and the fire of her love. This is a tale of unhappy disconnection.

In order to feel whole, complete, happy, successful and prosperous, we need to embrace both the yin and the yang within. We contain both yin and yang essences within us. Yet we will feel more at home with one or the other; this has nothing to do with gender – it is about essence. Masculine energy is assertive and action oriented. It's the energy we use to move through the world and to get things done. Masculine energy seeks to penetrate and understand the world and make things happen. Feminine energy is open and receptive; it is the energy of attraction and allowing. It is the energy we use to connect with the world, to relate with others, to build networks and to nurture the life force. Feminine energy seeks to embrace the world, to feel it and, in turn, to protect it.

A man comes into real intimate connection with his inner feminine, his anima, when he connects to his body, to his capacity for feeling, for his needs and vulnerability and for relating. A woman comes into alignment with her inner masculine, her animus, when she opens to the realm of being more decisive, focused, action oriented and independent. A man or woman with a strong masculine essence feels fulfilled and happy when they are aligned with their purpose. A man or woman with a strong feminine essence feels fulfilled and happy through being in authentic connection with others. The feminine is concerned with the soul of being, the masculine with the spirit of becoming. Both are necessary for a successful and happy life. The soulful life brings a deep satisfaction from the core of our being. The spirit-filled life is about diving into the fire of making things happen. The way of the lover is one of balance. The feminine person must embrace their masculine strength and power in order to help serve their feminine essence. The masculine person must seek out their inner softness and deep feelings and align them with their purpose. To be prosperous we do not need to look outside ourselves; we contain all the energies that we need.

There are many stories that speak of the masculine and the feminine. The fairy story of Beauty and the Beast is one example of the attraction between the two. The beast is horrific, frightening but lonely, gentle in his deepest nature. Beauty is sweet and lovely but unaware of her depths. Their story is one of union, a blending of fierceness with gentleness and sensitivity. It is about the power of sexual attraction. The person that denies their sexual energy also denies the creative force that creates and shapes the universe. Sexual attraction is the force that draws the masculine and the feminine into union. Sexual attraction can be a wake-up call to connect with ourselves in a deeper way.

Embracing the Other

Are you a masculine man or a feminine woman? Or are you a feminine man or a masculine woman? Do you find it easy to be (yang) active, outward looking, assertive, decisive, thinking, and action oriented? Or do you find it easy to be (yin) still, inward looking, reflective, intuitive, emotional and dreamy? Are you primarily a yin or a yang person?

Examine your beliefs about gender roles. What messages did you receive around gender as you were growing up? Look at your judgements about your non-primary energy. These are clues as to why you identify with the opposite pole.

Yin people need to: embrace thinking, planning, deciding, a sense of order and doing. Do something physical each day. Practise speaking out. Stretch and explore new ways of doing in the outer world.

Yang people need to: embrace feeling, stillness, a sense of chaos, and pure being. Meditate each day. Practise silence. Find new ways to gain awareness of the inner world.

Prosperity = Owning our Light

Facing our disowned light, beauty and hidden potential is scarier than facing our darkness, ugliness, shame, fear, doubt and so on. We have been taught from a young age to be afraid of our own light. We have been taught not to be too smart, too bright, too creative, too outspoken, too talented, or too gorgeous. In the process, we learn to be mediocre.

Because we do not want to look at our own giftedness, we tend to see this light shadow manifest in people around us whom we think are so wonderful in comparison with ourselves. The reason people fall in love with TV personalities and other celebrities is that they hold our light shadows. Many people unconsciously worship celebrities and do not realize that the qualities they see in these people are really their own, albeit as yet unrealized. Unconscious celebrity worship is a form of escapism. In the Great Depression, people found escape in Hollywood through idolizing stars like Clark Gable and Jean Harlow. Today, people lose themselves in mindless reality TV. Light shadow work is a conscious facing of all the gorgeous and talented people in the world and seeing them as a mirror of ourselves. The light shadow is reflected in all the intimates and people we meet that attract us. Sometimes the light shadow is also held by people who repel us.

The shadow can be revealed through a mixture of both attraction and repulsion. We may love and hate the people who reflect the light shadow. Perhaps we have a disowned warrior that another reflects, or a magician. We may have disowned our spirituality and see it reflected in another. We may have disowned our enthusiasm, our courage, our genius, or our passion. There is a wonderful saying that goes, 'If you spot it, you've got it.' All the gifts that you see in others are yours; you have come to awaken and share them with others on the planet.

Donna had a spiritual teacher who held her light shadow. Donna felt this teacher was so special, so wise, so insightful and so talented. After several years with her, Donna began to realize that she was a reflection of her own light shadow. In part, this was because the teacher was indeed wise and encouraged her students to examine the reflections of their dark and light shadows. Donna started embracing these same qualities in herself and, in time, began to be a spiritual teacher; being insightful and wise, she encouraged her students to examine the light and dark reflections in their reality.

Stephen fell in love with a young actress who was beautiful, talented, and also unavailable. He was able to see beyond the attraction to the qualities that she possessed. This helped him to handle the passion he felt for her without being driven mad. He spent some years working on finding in himself the qualities that she represented. He found that he had a certain power of presence. Although he never wanted to go on stage, he used this quality to good effect in the business world. In time, his feelings of passion subsided and they remained good friends. She no longer reflected his light shadow. Several years later, she shared with Stephen that she had always admired him and loved his power of presence. She could see in Stephen the things which he could not initially see in himself.

Owning the Light Shadow

Imagine that all the bright, gorgeous and talented people you see in the world are reflections for your own light shadow.

What qualities do you greatly admire in others? What celebrities do you find attractive? Why? Think of three great role models in this life. What gifts do they possess that are clues to your own? Think of three characters from history that you would like to have met. What qualities do you see in these people?

Men – what other men do you admire? Why? What women do you admire? Why?

Women – what other women do you admire? Why? What men do you admire? Why?

Imagine standing in front of a mirror in which you can see all the people you admire. One by one, reclaim the gifts that you see in them and own them in yourself. You could say, 'I see the gift of courage in you and I reclaim that gift as my own.'

Prosperity = A Sacred Marriage

Prosperity is a sacred marriage between yin and yang. In Ancient India these polarities were considered deities. Shakti and Shiva have been worshiped for thousands of years. Shakti is the feminine principle that represents the substance of all of manifest creation; the gateway to Shakti is the base chakra. Shakti is the power that creates, preserves, destroys and recreates the universe.

Shiva, the male principle, represents the bliss of pure consciousness; the gateway to Shiva is through the crown chakra. Shiva is seen as being both static and dynamic and as both creator and destroyer. He is the oldest and the youngest. He is omnipresent and resides in everyone as pure consciousness. Shiva is often depicted standing on a tiger's skin, for this represents the dominion of the mind. According to Tantric texts, 'Only when Shiva is united with Shakti does he have the power to create'.

The lover embraces the feminine pole of the body, emotions and earth and also the masculine pole of will, intellect and consciousness. In this union there is no lack on the inside; all dormant talents and abilities are embraced and nurtured. This union creates a prosperous life on earth and a rich spiritual life. Shiva is inseparable from Shakti. There is no Shiva without Shakti and no Shakti without Shiva; the two are one entwined in a state of being and non-being, in consciousness and bliss.

Prosperity = Embracing Yin

Shakti energy is a container of prosperity. In Hindu mythology, the goddess Lakshmi is the patron of wealth and good fortune on earth. Her four hands represent four aspects of human life: *dharma* or right living, *kama* or desires, *artha* or wealth, and *moksha* or liberation from the cycle of birth and death. Cascades of gold coins flow from her hands. Her gold-embroidered red robe symbolizes the activities of prosperity. Both householders and businessmen offer prayers to her for their wellbeing and for the prosperity of their family and commercial undertakings. She is seated on a lotus because wealth is linked with the fertilizing powers of moist soil and the mysterious powers of growth.

The earth is in such a sorry state because we have forgotten to call on the power of the earth for assistance. Instead of connecting with the earth, we have sought to plunder it. The scarcity game creates a terrible sense of disconnection from the earth. For many centuries, we have lived within a grand limiting mythology of God being a distant father-landlord figure. This is the myth of transcendent dominance. In this myth, the distant landlord sends messengers to post lists of do's and don'ts to let people know how to behave. There is also the ever-present threat of eternal punishment for those that ignore the rules.

The lover embraces a very different mythology: one of immanence. There is a Shinto saying that says, 'Even in a single leaf of a tree or a tender blade of grass, the awe-inspiring Deity manifests Itself.' The lover walks the path of immanence and sees divine power as existing within all living things. Nothing is separate or cast out. The myth of immanence is the one in which all indigenous peoples live. The lover lives within the myth where we are still in the sacred garden, where we were never thrown out of paradise. The lover stands in the garden and lives within a universe that cares about his or her existence and growth. The path of the lover is one of connection and Oneness. Physical existence is a divine state. The body and feelings are sacred temples that allow the soul expression in this world. The way of the lover is about finding meaning, belonging and a home in the world. The lover has a relational outlook and does not see a world of separate, free-floating and unrelated objects. The lover is not interested in escaping from the world but in connecting with it more intimately. The way of embracing immanent yin is a path of growth through joy and delight. Suffering is about being thrown out of the garden. Suffering is the way of sin and punishment. This myth is not the way of the lover. The lover sees the divine in all things – within a glorious sunrise, a daffodil on a cool spring day, a wave crashing upon a golden beach, a child's smile, and within the reflective other. The divine is the power that causes the sun to shine, the rain to fall, and the seeds to grow. There is a Deeper Intelligence at work in all life. If only we would stop for a moment to feel it...

The lover is like a bee that collects the things that bring joy: all else is dropped. The lover gives no energy to old stories that maintain painful realities. The lover uses the temple of the body to stay grounded within the yin energy of the world. They walk within the embrace of Mother Earth, they walk in wild places and are open to the rousing power of the elements. It is through connection to the earth that this deep cleansing takes place. The lover honours the gifts of the earth. The earth is abundant and creative; all wealth comes from her treasure house. All the precious jewels and metals come from Her. All the things we eat and drink are gifts from the earth.

A lover is as happy being alone as with other people. Lovers need space to regenerate because they live so fully. The lover is a child of the earth and stars and knows no bounds – a free spirit who loves self and life and the source of all existence. The path of the lover is a spiritual path. Some spiritual paths such as Sufism talk about love, of paradise, and the divine in the same breath. Sufis regard God as the Beloved. They abandon themselves in dance and song to the divine impulse. Sufism is a yin path or receptive path because it opens to the divine rather than actively seeking it out. The way of the lover is the path of poetry and dance. Rumi, an early Sufi Master, lived life as a dance. It is said that he attained to his first *samadhi* by dancing continuously for thirty-six hours. He danced with such ecstasy that by the time he reached his ultimate *samadhi*, thousands of people were dancing around him. He fell on the ground and remained still for hours. When he opened his eyes, he looked out on a different world.

The Path to Shakti

Sit or lie in a quiet space. Relax your body and start to take some long, slow, conscious breaths.

Then start to ground into the earth by imagining roots growing out of your feet or the base of your spine and pushing down on each out breath. Send these roots right down to the core of the earth.

Just below your feet, an energy centre begins to open. Like an earthly sun, this power shines in the earth. In this centre sleeps the Shakti energy of the earth. This energy is depicted as a sleeping serpent. It can be seen as streams of light. With each breath imagine breathing up this energy.

Breathe it into the base chakra and open to your physical identity.
Breathe it into the sacral chakra and open to your emotional identity.
Breathe it into the solar plexus chakra and open to your intellectual identity.
Breathe it into the heart chakra and open to your loving identity.

Open to the love of the earth. Anchor this current in your heart. Feel yourself expanding in this intimate embrace. All precious things come from the earth. Open to the healing and wealthy touch of nature.

Prosperity = Embracing Yang

Long ago in a distant land, there was a large Buddha statue made of pure gold. It was as high as ten people and sat in a lotus position in the beautiful and tranquil garden of a Buddhist monastery. Over the years, many people came to sit at its feet and pray or meditate. In time, a great marauding army invaded the country and the community of monks decided to disguise their beloved statue so that it looked like ordinary stone. They worked tirelessly until the whole statue was covered with grey cement. When the army passed the monastery, they paid the statue no attention. The army occupied the land for many years and, by the time they left, everyone had forgotten the true nature of the statue. One day, as a young man went to meditate under the statue, a piece of cement fell off revealing its true nature. Soon, the local people were alerted and the statue was restored to its original golden condition. This golden statue still sits in its original position in a garden in The Temple of the Golden Buddha in Bangkok.

The lover seeks altered consciousness not just to create miracles but to enter into a direct union with God. The Shiva force is a descending current of love. The lover embraces the current of descending force and is open to the embrace of spirit. The danger and wonder of this is that opening to the higher vibration of love will start to shatter the illusions of the scarcity game. This is dangerous, for we might stop worrying about our pensions and retirement and live completely in the present moment!

Shiva is pure consciousness, undifferentiated bliss, unified with all that is. He shapes primordial chaos into order and form. He is also the Lord of Destruction, who destroys our attachments, and the Lord of Sleep, who brings night dreams and waking visions. He is the vastness of the imagination and the bringer of enlightenment. The transcendent spirit is known by many names; in the spiritual tradition of India it is called the Atman which means 'breath', or 'vital principle'. The Atman is our personal guiding spirit. The Atman resides in Brahman, the Universal Intelligence that sustains all things. In Hawaii, the personal spirit is known as Aumakua which translates as 'utterly trustworthy parental self'. The transcendent spirit is also known as Buddha Mind, Christ Consciousness, Deep Self, Holy Guardian Angel or Higher Self. Spirit is the descending force of consciousness that seeks to enter ever more deeply into matter. Opening to this force is like finding a great treasure, for this transcendent spirit illuminates the way to what we are becoming. This is the current of enlightenment, wisdom and guidance. Shakti creates the forms for Shiva to inhabit. Shiva enters these forms and enlivens them.

This current liberates us from our prisons of limiting perception and fear. It can help us to lead a truly abundant life in that we no longer feel dependent on external objects, people or circumstances in order to feel prosperous. Prosperity does not lie outside of the self; we are the source of our prosperity. This same message has been repeated by spiritual teachers throughout the ages. The Master Jesus in the New Testament said, 'the kingdom of heaven is like a merchant looking for fine pearls. When he found one of great value, he went away and sold everything he had and bought it.' Opening to spirit does not mean that we become an ascetic; the spiritual life is a prosperous one for prosperity exists within the fibre of our being. Prosperity is the Intelligence that sustains the Universe. The same power that holds the earth in its orbit around the sun can help you in your life. This Higher Power is very willing and able to be of help. It will not, however, interfere in our lives but will assist when asked. Assistance does not always come in the way that we expect.

The Path to Shiva

Sit or lie in a quiet space. Relax your body and start to take some long, slow, conscious breaths.

Just above your head, an energy centre begins to open. Like a brilliant sun, the soul star radiates the power of the cosmos. In this centre is our awakening consciousness, the Shiva energy of the cosmos. Within the radiant light of the soul star, see an opening eye. From its gaze pours down a current of light; with each breath, imagine breathing down this energy.

Breathe this light down into the crown chakra and open to your spiritual identity.
Breathe this light down into the third eye chakra and open to your archetypal identity.
Breathe this light down into the throat chakra and open to your creative identity.
Breathe this light down into the heart chakra and open to your social identity.

Open to the awakening power of the spirit. Anchor this current in your heart. Feel yourself expanding in this intimate embrace. From the cosmos comes higher guidance and the ability to create a heaven on earth.

Divine Union in the Heart

Consciously invite the ascending current of Shakti into your heart. Open to the loving embrace of the earth.

Consciously invite the descending current of Shiva into your heart. Open to the loving embrace of the cosmos.

See these two forces unite inside of you. Feel them set your heart on fire with bliss. Feel this fire burn around your energy field cleansing, protecting and invigorating you.

Shakti is a wild and ecstatic energy, the dance of life, the wildness of nature, the throb of drums that awaken the dance. Shiva is a peaceful and graceful current. In the sacred marriage of Shakti and Shiva lies the possibility of true abundance and prosperity. Shiva without Shakti is disembodied and unconnected to the physical realm. Shakti without Shiva has no possibility of redemption from the binding forces of matter. Yet, when they embrace, the energies unite in an orgasmic dance which lights up the cosmos; life becomes juicy, and the impossible possible. The person that unites Shakti and Shiva within their form becomes magnetic to their higher good. In this state, reality appears to be less solid and impenetrable and more malleable.

Prosperity = A Deep Surrender

There is an old tale of a man who was walking along a cliff. He fell over the edge and hurtled towards the rocks below. Fortunately, he had his wits about him and he managed to grab a branch on the way down and stop his fall. When he looked up, the way back seemed impossible. When he looked down, he saw certain death. Having no idea of how to escape, he called out, 'Is anyone there?' His voice echoed into the distance but there was no answer. He called out again, 'Is anyone there?' and listened for an answer but all was still and silent. He called out for a third and final time, 'Is anyone there?' And this time a great and beautiful voice answered as if coming from everywhere and nowhere at the same time. 'If you let go of the branch, I will send two of my angels to catch you and bring you to a new place of safety.' The man thought for a moment; he was very tired. He took a breath, waited a moment, and then said clearly and loudly, 'Is anybody else there?'

The word surrender is often thought of as a weakness, a giving up, a letting another have their way, an admission of defeat. Surrender is not about giving into the demands of another but a release into love itself.

Love is the glue that binds life together. The lover does not surrender to anything other than love. To do so would feel like a betrayal of the authentic self. This surrender is a movement into our deepest truth. Real surrender goes beyond the concerns of the personality, it is something that concerns the soul. The soul knows union with the universe. Union is a dropping of all personal limitation and a release into the vastness of creation.

The way of the lover is to surrender but this is not easy. There are times when it seems that we have little choice but to surrender, yet we often hesitate. The ultimate act of the lover is to surrender, not to another person or a false guru but to life itself. We must surrender because ultimately nothing belongs to us; everything in life is on loan. Each breath we take is on loan and we cannot hold on to the life force that keeps our hearts beating. We will take none of our possessions with us when we die; we will leave all our projects behind for others to discard, continue or complete. We will leave all our money behind. Perhaps it will bring pleasure to others, perhaps not. The scarcity mentality does not allow us to surrender. Scarcity tells us to hold on and not lose the things we have struggled so hard to achieve and possess. The prosperity mindset tells us to surrender so that we may gain so much more.

Prosperity is a ongoing meditation or a deep prayer. The key to prayer is, first of all, to have a heartfelt request and then to surrender that request to the Higher Power in the universe. This means letting go of how that desired outcome will come about.

When Jane was at boarding school, she felt very isolated and lonely. She reached rock bottom one day and got down on her knees to pray. In that instant she felt 'a warm column of energy' flow around her and knew that her prayer had been answered. Less than a minute afterwards, someone knocked on her door. She opened it to find a young woman of the same age who invited her out to dinner. That was the turning point; from then on she made many friends. The young woman who knocked at her door remained a life-long friend.

Lis was feeling temporarily hard up and in desperate need of a holiday. At a personal development training seminar, she stood up and shared that she really needed a good break. A few weeks later, a friend unexpectedly offered to pay for her to join her on holiday in Thailand. Later, Lis sent a prayer to the universe to help her get some spending money. At the airport there was a problem with her flight and the airline offered to pay her over £400 for the inconvenience. At the last minute, her prayer was answered.

Susan had accrued several thousand pounds of debt during a period of being self-employed. She decided that she wanted to clear her debts and knew that she did not want to 'do it the long and hard way'. She started to form a strong intention and began to release prayers to her 'angels and guides' to help show her the way. Nothing happened until she decided to take some positive action. She phoned a debt management phone line and, when she got off the phone and went down stairs to go out, she noticed that the post had arrived. She opened the mail and found a cheque for £10,000 from a relative who wanted to give her a gift.

Robert worked for a charity where there was a lot of conflict. This conflict had been going on for several months and the charity was heading for serious financial trouble. Some key staff members resigned and Robert was appointed as a director. Although the conflict had ended with the resignations, he was not sure how the organization could survive; it barely had enough money to pay the remaining staff for another month. All he could do was pray for a financial miracle. Within two weeks, Robert had a call from a person who had just inherited a large amount of money and wanted to donate several thousand pounds to the charity. This amount was enough to help the charity through a very difficult period.

Chris was divorcing her husband and the family home was being sold. She was looking for a house so that she could have her sons back to live with her. Every house she looked at was awful; nothing she saw came close to what she had imagined. Time was running out. The family home had been sold and the new owners were moving in two weeks' time. Chris was feeling under pressure. Suddenly she got an inspiration. She sat bolt upright in bed and spoke out loud into the darkness. 'I would like a home for my two sons and me, one that has three good-sized bedrooms, a living room, a kitchen and a dining room. I would like this home to be within my price range. I want to be able to afford it. And I would like it to be clean, spacious, light and airy.' She sank back down and was about to go to sleep when she remembered to say something else, 'Oh, and if I have a choice, I would like this house to be in the Hamilton Road and Bulmershe Road area.' Then she fell into a deep sleep. The next day, she was looking in estate agents' windows when her mobile phone rang. It was an estate agent with whom she hadn't registered. They asked her if she was still looking for a house and went on to describe one that had just come on the market that very day. It had 3 good-sized bedrooms, a living room that was light and airy, a newly refurbished kitchen/dining room and it was in her price bracket. What was even better was that it had been a rental property and the owner wanted to sell it but was willing to rent it to Chris until the sale went through. She was astounded by this news. The estate agent then said that it was on a development that sat between Hamilton Road and Bulmershe Road!

I was working hard yet money seemed to be flowing faster away from me than towards me. I felt a that 'this should not be happening to me.' I decided to send a prayer to the Universe which went something like, 'if writing this book is meant to be my path then please give me a sign involving more money flowing into my life within the next few days.' Within 48 hours a friend contacted me looking for a particular something. I was able to help her out and suddenly an unexpected £500 flowed into my life. Within a week another similar amount unexpectedly flowed in. My prayer was answered. I continued writing this book!

Eastern poets describe human souls as drops of water that will eventually dissolve into the ocean of God. Another way to look at this is to see that the drop of water can open to the ocean; instead of just dissolving away we remain conscious of who we are in this life and thereby access the mystery and power of the greater ocean of consciousness. Prosperity is how the universe works. Real prosperity comes from learning to rest and trust in the source of life. The same power and intelligence that gives birth to stars and galaxies and sustains worlds in their orbits is there to help us in our everyday affairs.

The Source does not interfere with our lives but is there to support and sustain us if we are willing to open our hearts and minds and soul to this power. To connect with Source, we have to undertake the journey. We have to activate and use the gifts with which we came into this world. These resources are doorways into the divine. No amount of begging or pleading will cajole the Source to help us in our journey. Beneath begging and pleading lies the idea that we are not connected with the Source. The paradox is that we are never separate from the Source no matter how much we believe we are, and no matter what we do to maintain this illusion. We are not separate from the creator and sustainer of all things. When we really experience this, we will experience grace and create miracles for ourselves and others.

The Baha'i Method of Prayer

1. Pray and ask for guidance around something that you want to create. Then remain in the silence of contemplation for a few minutes.

2. In silent contemplation, be open to being shown the next step. Then decide to take step three.

3. Have determination to carry through what has been shown. Otherwise, what you want will remain a vague longing.

4. Have faith and confidence that the power will flow through you; that the right way will appear; that the door will open; that the right thought, the right message, the right principle, or the right book will be given to you. Have confidence and the right thing will come to your need. Then, as you rise from prayer, take the fifth step at once.

5. Act as though your prayer has already been granted. Act with tireless, ceaseless energy. As you act, you yourself will become a magnet which will attract more power to your being, until you become an unobstructed channel through which the divine power can flow.

It is my prayer that your journey through this lifetime be a blessed, enlightening and prosperous one.

Steve Nobel

The Heart Led Life

This book may now be ended
But your journey's just begun
These words they are intended
As a cosmic starters gun
For though life's not a race now
And the scenic rout is best
You're ready with the know how
To forge a world that's blessed
So arise your warrior self
Let courage lead the way
And bring you to that wealth
That's born when fear's at bay
Awaken now the lover-you
Who's yearning deep inside
To know the glow that other do
Who brave the heart led ride
That magician who is dancing
With your visions in her hand
Is the one that you see glancing
In the mirror where you stand
The love that pulses through your veins
When passion's tides are high
Now asks for you to take the reins
And let your soul birds fly.

Eliza Kenyon

Recommended Reading

Abram, David. *The Spell of the Sensuous.* Vintage, 1997

Adrienne, Carol. *When Life Changes or You Wish it Would.* HarperCollins, 2003

Allen, David. *Getting Things Done.* Piatkus, 2002

Anand, Margo. *The Art of Sexual Magic.* Piatkus, 2003

Bach, Richard. *Illusions.* Mandarin, 1992

Block, Peter. *Stewardship.* Berrett Koehler, 1996

Bly, Robert and Woodman, Marion. *The Maiden King.* HarperCollins, 1999

Bolchover, David. *The Living Dead: Switched Off, Zoned Out.* Capstone Publishing Ltd, 2005

Boyle, David. *The Little Money Book.* Alistair Sawday Publishing, 2003

Brown Jr, Tom. *The Tracker.* Berkley Publishing Group, 1996

Bruges, James. *The Little Earth Book.* Alistair Sawday Publishing, 2004

Bunting, Madeleine. *Willing Slaves.* Harper Perennial, 2005

Buzan, Tony. *Embracing Change.* BBC Books, 2005

—. *The Mind Map Book.* BBC Active, 2003

Cameron, Julia. *The Artist's Way.* Pan Books, 1995

Campbell, Joseph. *The Hero with a Thousand Faces.* Princeton Univ. Press, 1990

—. *The Masks of God: Primitive Mythology.* Souvenir Press Ltd, 1973

Capra, Fritjof. *The Hidden Connections.* Flamingo, 2003

Carroll, Lenedra J. *The Architecture of All Abundance.* Piatkus, 2005

Covey, Stephen R. *The Seven Habits of Highly Effective People.* Simon & Schuster, 1990

Czikszentmihalyi, Mihaly. *Flow.* Rider & Co., 2002

Deida, David. *The Way of the Superior Man.* Sounds True, 2004

Dooley, Mike. *Notes from the Universe.* Totally Unique Thoughts, 2003

Edwards, Gill. *Living Magically.* Piatkus, 1999

Feinstein, David; Eden, Donna; and Craig, Gary. *The Healing Power of EFT and Energy* Psychology. Piatkus, 2006

Gall, John. *The Systems Bible*. General Systemantics Press, 2003

Gibran, Kahlil. *The Prophet*. Pan Books, 1991

Handy, Charles. *The Hungry Spirit: Beyond Capitalism*. Arrow, 1998

Hansen, Mark Victor. *The One Minute Millionaire*. Vermilion, 2002

Hay, Louise L. *You Can Heal Your Life*. Hay House, 2002

Hendricks, Gay and Ludeman, Kate. *The Corporate Mystic*. Bantam, 1997

Holden, Robert. *Success Intelligence*. Hodder Mobius, 2005

Ingerman, Sandra. *Medicine for the Earth*. Random House USA, 2001

—. *Soul Retrieval*. Harper San Francisco, 1991

Judith, Anodea. *Eastern Body, Western Mind*. Celestial Arts, 2004

Katie, Byron. *Loving What Is*. Rider & Co., 2002

King, Serge Kahili. *Urban Shaman*. Simon & Schuster, 1991

Klinger, Sharon A. *Intuition and Beyond*. Rider & Co., 2002

Kornfield, Jack. *A Path with Heart*. Rider & Co., 2002

Krystal, Phyllis. *Cutting the Ties that Bind*. Redwheel / Weiser, 1993

Ladinsky, Daniel (translator). *The Gift: Poems by Hafiz*. Penguin Compass, 1999

Lansley, Stewart. *Rich Britain: The Rise and Rise of the Super-Wealthy*. Politico's Publishing Ltd, 2006

Moore, Robert and Gillette, Douglas. *King, Warrior, Magician,* Lover. Harper SanFrancisco, 1991

Murphy, Joseph. *The Power of the Subconscious Mind*. Pocket Books, 2006

Newton, Peter. *The Middle Path of Tai Chi*. Findhorn Press, 2005

O'Connor, Joseph. *NLP Workbook*. HarperCollins, 2001

Orman, Suze. *The Laws of Money*. Hay House, 2005

Roberts, Jane. *The Nature of Personal Reality (a Seth book)*. Amber Allen, 1994

Roman, Sanaya and Packer, Duane. *Creating Money*. H.J. Kramer, 1988

Roman, Sanaya. *Spiritual Growth*. H.J. Kramer Inc., 1989

Rosenberg, Marshall. *Non-violent Communication*. Puddle Dancer Press, 2003

Schumacher, E.F. *Small is Beautiful*. Vintage, 1993

Starhawk. *The Earth Path*. HarperCollins, 2005

—. *The Spiral Dance.* Harper San Francisco, 1999

Stone, Hal and Sidra. *Embracing Our Selves.* Nataraj Publishing, 1993

—. *Embracing Your Inner Critic.* Harper San Francisco, 1993

Twist, Lynne. *The Soul of Money.* W.W. Norton & Co. Ltd, 2003

Villoldo, Alberto. *Mending the Past, Healing the Future.* Hay House, 2005

—. *Shaman,* Healer, Sage. Bantam, 2001

Walsch, Neale Donald. *Conversations with God.* Hodder & Stoughton, 1997

Wanless, James. *Voyager Tarot.* Merrill West Publishing, 1992

Wenger, Win and Poe, Richard. *The Einstein Factor.* Crown Publications, 2003

Wheen, Francis. *How Mumbo Jumbo Conquered the World.* Harper Perennial, 2004

Whyte, David. *Crossing the Unknown Sea.* Penguin, 2001

Williams, Nick. *How to Be Inspired.* Tethered Camel, 2005

—. *The Work We Were Born To Do.* Element, 2000

Wiseman, Richard. *The Luck Factor.* Arrow, 2004

Zohar, Danah. *Spiritual Capital.* Bloomsbury, 2005

Useful Websites

The Author:

    www.prosperitygame.co.uk – Steve Nobel, London

General – Business:

    www.nick-williams.com – Heart at Work, London

    www.davidwhyte.com – Many Rivers, USA

    www.mbnlp.com – MBNLP, London

General – Healing

    www.shamanismworks.co.uk – Energy Healing, London

General – Money:

    www.letslinkuk.org – Lets UK

    www.moneysavingexpert.com – Money Saving Expert, UK

    www.neweconomics.org – New Economics Foundation, London

    www.prosperityuk.com – Prosperity, UK

    www.themoneyshaman.com – The Money Shaman, UK

    www.soulofmoney.org – The Soul of Money, USA

    www.triodos.co.uk – Triodos Bank, UK

General – Personal Development:

    www.alternatives.org.uk – Alternatives, London

    www.essence-foundation.com – Essence Foundation, London

    www.findhorn.org – Findhorn Foundation, Scotland.

    www.happiness.co.uk – Happiness Project, London

General – Publications:

    www.caduceus.info – Caduceus Magazine, UK

    www.positivenews.org.uk – Positive News Magazine, UK

    www.resurgence.org – Resurgence Magazine, UK

    www.theecologist.co.uk – The Ecologist Magazine, UK

The Way of the Seer:

www.collegeofpsychicstudies.co.uk – College of Psychic Studies, London

The Way of the Warrior:

www.mkp.org.uk – Mankind Project, UK

The Way of the Magician:

www.thefourwinds.com – Four Winds Society, USA

www.livingmagically.co.uk – Living Magically, Cumbria, UK

www.medicinefortheearth.com – Medicine for the Earth, USA

www.sacredcenters.com – Sacred Centres, USA

The Way of the Lover:

www.diamondlighttantra.com – Diamond White Tantra, UK

www.schoolofawakening.com – School of Awakening, UK

Acknowledgements

Grateful acknowledgement is made to Gill Edwards for permission to quote from *Living Magically,* and to the Publishing Department, Visva-Bharati University, for permission to quote from *The Songs of Kabir* by Rabindranath Tagore.

There are so many people who have helped to shape this book, more than I can mention here. I would like to thank Gill for holding up a torch and being a bright light; Ashley for showing me the trickster; Brian for his amazing wisdom; David for his creativity and courage; Michael for his corporate brilliance; Nick for his vision around work; Menis for his systemic understanding and great heart; Ollie for his strength; Hal and Sidra for handing me the keys to the psyche; Alberto, Jonathon and Starhawk for being my guides in the magical realms; Sue and David for their friendship; and Lazaris, Orin, DaBen and Seth for showing me that living joyfully and effectively in the world is possible and wonderful.

I would like to thank my many friends at Alternatives, both old and new. Alternatives has shown me that another world is not only possible but necessary. I would like to thank Ursula for her inner beauty and Ian, Lynda and Peter for their ability to keep me grounded in everyday reality. And last but not least I would like to thank all the visionary people at Findhorn Press for their faith in publishing this book.

FINDHORN
Press

*Books, Card Sets,
CDs & DVDs
that inspire and uplift*

For a complete catalogue,
please contact:

Findhorn Press Ltd
305a The Park, Findhorn
Forres IV36 3TE
Scotland, UK

Telephone
+44-(0)1309-690582
Fax
+44-(0)1309-690036
eMail
info@findhorpress.com

or consult our catalogue online
(with secure order facility) on

www.findhornpress.com